Cover Shot: Alfonso Petrire
Surfer: Manu Carrique at P

Copyright © 2010 Blue Planet Surf Maps, Inc.

ISBN # 9781441407559

No part of this publication may be reproduced, stored in a retrieval system or transmitted in any form or by any means, electronic, mechanical, photocopying, recording, scanning or otherwise, except as permitted under Sections 107 or 108 of the 1976 United States Copyright Act, without either the prior written permission of the Pu lisher, or authorization through payment of the appropriate per-copy fee .

Trademarks: Blue Planet Surf Maps, the Blue Planet Surf Maps logo, and related trade dress are trademarks or registered trademarks of Blue Planet Surf Maps, Inc., in the United States and other countries,and may not be used without written permission. All other trademarks are the property of their respective owners. Wiley Publishing, Inc., is not associated with any product or vendor mentioned in this book is a trademark of Blue Planet Surf Maps, Inc.

LIMIT OF LIABILITY/DISCLAIMER OF WARRANTY:WHILE THE PUBLISHER AND AUTHOR HAVE USED THEIR BEST EFFORTS IN PREPARING THIS BOOK,THEY MAKE NO REPRESENTATIONS OR WARRANTIES WITH RESPECT TO THE ACCURACY OR COMPLETENESS OF THE CONTENTS OF THIS BOOK AND SPECIFICALLY DISCLAIM ANY IMPLIED WARRANTIES OF MERCHANTABILITY OR FITNESS FOR A PARTICULAR PURPOSE.NO WARRANTY MAY BE CREATED OR EXTENDED BY SALES REPRESENTATIVES OR WRITTEN SALES MATERIALS.THE ADVICE AND STRATEGIES CONTAINED HEREIN MAY NOT BE SUITABLE FOR YOUR SITUATION. YOU SHOULD CONSULT WITH A PROFESSIONAL WHERE APPROPRIATE.NEITHER THE PUBLISHER NOR AUTHOR SHALL BE LIABLE FOR ANY LOSS OF PROFIT OR ANY OTHER COMMERCIAL DAMAGES,INCLUDING BUT NOT LIMITED TO SPECIAL,I NCIDENTAL,CONSEQUENTIAL,OR OTHER DAMAGES.

The Essential Surfing
COSTA RICA
Guide & Surf Map Set

3rd Edition

SPECIAL THANKS TO:

Our Families and Friends, Alacran Surf Tours, Cala Luna
www.surf-costarica.com,

Table of Contents

INTRODUCTION 6
    Surfing in Costa Rica 8
    Map of Surfing Regions 9
    When to Go 14
    What to Bring 15

TRANSPORTATION
    Flying In 16
    Buses 18
    Renting a Car 19
    In-Country Flights 20

SURFING COSTA
    Map of Costa Surf Spots 21
    Surf Spots in General 23
    Renting a Car 15
    In-Country Flights 16

NORTH PACIFIC SURF SPOTS
    Map of North Pacific Spots 12
    Tamarindo Surf Spots 14
    North of Tamarindo 15
    South of Tamarindo 16
    Nosara Surf Spots 16
    Mal Pais/Santa Teresa 16

CENTRAL PACIFIC SURF SPOTS
    Map of North Pacific Spots 12
    Tamarindo Surf Spots 14
    North of Tamarindo 15
    South of Tamarindo 16
    Nosara Surf Spots 16
    Mal Pais/Santa Teresa 16

Table of Contents continued.

SOUTH PACIFIC SURF SPOTS
- Map of North Pacific Spots — 12
- Tamarindo Surf Spots — 14
- North of Tamarindo — 15
- South of Tamarindo — 16
- Nosara Surf Spots — 16
- Mal Pais/Santa Teresa — 16

CARIBBEAN SURF SPOTS
- Map of North Pacific Spots — 12
- Tamarindo Surf Spots — 14
- North of Tamarindo — 15
- South of Tamarindo — 16
- Nosara Surf Spots — 16
- Mal Pais/Santa Teresa — 16

INTRODUCTION: SURFING IN COSTA RICA

Intro to Costa Rica

COSTA RICA is an amazing place for a surf trip. Costa Rica is a well known and well developed surfing destination - especially since featuring in Endless Summer 2; direct flights from the USA also add to its popularity. The country is relatively safe, beautiful, friendly and blessed with great surfing on both coasts. It is, however one of the more expensive countries in the central and south Americas, with the positive aspect that hotels are good quality and car rental relatively easy and safe.

The surfing can be broken into four main areas: The Pacific North (Guanacaste-Nicoya, Tamarindo, Nosara, Mal Pais), the Pacific Centrel (Puntareans, Jaco and Dominical area) the Pacific South (Osa Peninsula, Pavones) and the Caribbean (Cahuita, Puerto Viejo). Surf towns are developing in places such as Jaco, Tamarindo and Puerto Viejo. Year round warm water, warm air and offshore breezes (in Guanacaste in Northern Costa Rica) make for great conditions. The best waves occur in the rainy season (northern Hemisphere 'summer') on the pacific side.

North of Costa Rica is Nicaragua, another great country for surfing, es-

INTRODUCTION: SURFING IN COSTA RICA

pecially around the San Juan del Sur area, which is conveniently located not for from the Costa Rican border on the Pacific Coast.

South of Costa Rica is Panama, which is yet another great surf destination. The surf in Panama is accessible on both sides same as Costa Rica. Both Panama and Nicaragua are considerably less expensive than Costa Rica. See our Nicaragua and Panama Surfing Guides for further information (www.blueplanetsurfmaps.com).

Costa Rica is located on the Central American isthmus, 10° North of the equator and 84° West of the Prime Meridian. It borders both the Caribbean Sea (to the east) and the North Pacific Ocean (to the west), with a total of 1,290 kilometers (802 mi) of coastline (212 km / 132 mi on the Caribbean coast and 1,016 km / 631 mi on the Pacific). It is about the size of West Virginia.

The highest point in the country is Cerro Chirripó, at 3,810 metres (12,500 ft), and is the fifth highest peak in Central America. The highest volcano in the country is the Irazú Volcano (3,431 m / 11,257 ft). The largest lake in Costa Rica is Lake Arenal.

Costa Rica also comprises several islands. Cocos Island stands out because of its distance from continental landmass (24 km^2 / 9.25 sq mi, 500 km or 300 mi (480 km) from Puntarenas coast), but Calero Island is the largest island of the country (151.6 km^2 / 58.5 sq mi).

Costa Rica protects 23% of its national territory within the Protected Areas system. It also possesses the greatest density of species in the world.

Advertise with Us - We give great deal to local businesses. Up to 75% off our rates.

When to Go

What can you expect with our weather and climate?

Costa Rica is a tropical country situated between 8 and 11 degrees above the equator. It has only two seasons: dry and wet. The dry season with very little rain is generally between late December and April and the green or wet season lasts the rest of the year - May through November, but still offers an average of about 5 hours of daily sunshine. The Caribbean coast doesen't have this extended dry weather and stays green all year round and due to the humidity, tends to be a little oppressive sometimes. The Central Mountainous Region is more temperate, like the spring-like weather in San Jose, the capital city.

Temperatures vary little between seasons. The main influence on temperature is altitude. San José at 1150m (3772ft) has a climate which the locals refer to as the "eternal Spring". Average temperature ranges in San Jose are from 14 to 24 degrees Celsius (57 to 75 degrees Fahrenheit) in December to 17 to 27 degrees Celsius (63 to 81 degrees Fahrenheit) in May.

At lower elevations, sea level coasts are much hotter, with the Caribbean averaging 21°C (70°F) at night and over 30°C (86°F) during the day. The Pacific side is a few degrees warmer still, but the humidity is generally less, so it tends to be more comfortable.

The Northern Pacific Region is referred to as the "Gold Coast" and has an abundance of large resort hotels because of the drier and sunnier climate. It is also referred to as the "Guanacaste Area". The area along the Central Pacific is greener, because of more rainfall, and then going more south toward Dominical and further, it rains more and is more humid. However, you can be quite comfortable in the lowlands weather of either side if you dress minimally and limit your exposure to the midday, intense tropical sun.

What's the wet season like?

In Costa Rica, that's the time of year when, for most of the country, you may get some rain during your travels. And, it's also the less crowded, off-peak season. Many people actually prefer to vacation during the wet season, as the pace is slower, it's easier to find hotel accommodations, the rates are less, and, of course, the surf is bigger! October is usually the rainiest month on the Pacific side, but you could be here for a week and see none, or you might see afternoon - night time showers, or perhaps several days of clouds and drizzle and rain. But, for most vacationers, there is eventually more than enough sun.

What about the Caribbean side?

The Caribbean side definitely surffers a bad rap from weather reporters.. While it is true that the Caribbean side of Costa Rica gets more rain, unfortunately the way that weather is reported makes it sound like it never stops raining there. The Caribbean is often reported as "raining in the Caribbean" when in reality, it is only raining in one of the micro-climates along the long seacoast, and the rest is perfectly sunny. Yes, it receives more rain than the arid "Gold Coast," almost always sunny northern Guanacaste Pacific coast, but for more lush vegetation, and most of the time nothing more than an afternoon shower, you will enjoy the verdant natural surroundings, flora and fauna of the uncrowded, laid back Caribbean side with epic waves. Oh, and one more thing, when it does rain in Costa Rica, at least it's a warm, tropical rain.

Swell & Weather

	Jan/Feb	Mar/Apr	May/Jun	Jul/Aug	Sep/Oct	Nov/Dec
SWELL SIZE (FEET):	3-5	4-5	5-7	6-7	5-6	3-4
SWELL DIRECTION:	S-SW	S-SW	S-SW	S-SW	S-SW	S-SW
CONSISTENCY:	FAIR	GOOD	GOOD	EXCELLENT	GOOD	FAIR
AIR TEMP:	26C° - 78F°	28C° - 86F°	27C° - 79F°	27C° - 79F°	27C° - 79F°	27C° - 79F°
WIND DIRECTION:	S-SE	S-SE	S-SE	S-SE	S-SE	S-SE
WETSUIT:	boardshorts	boardshorts	boardshorts	boardshorts	boardshorts	boardshorts
WATER TEMP:	27C° - 81F°	27C° - 81F°	27C° - 79F°	27C° - 79F°	27C° - 79F°	27C° - 79F°

Hurricane & Cyclone Forecasts

Hurricanes and Cyclones can hit either coast, so keep up date using the forecasting tools provided by National Hurricane Center at www.nhc.noaa.gov/ The 48 hour formation potential forecast for the Atlantic is available from June 1st to November 30, while the Pacific tracking system is available year-round.

INTRODUCTION: WHEN TO GO

Searching for Surf, Osa Peninsula
Photo: Thornten Cohn

What to Bring

- [ ] PASSPORT (Passport valid 6 months beyond intended stay)
- [ ] Extra Cash
- [ ] Surfboards
- [ ] Single Day Board Bag (this is a single board bag, not a sock; to ensure the safety or your board)
- [ ] Leashes
- [ ] Extra Fins (They're expensive and can be hard to find non FCS)
- [ ] Baggies
- [ ] Tropical Wax
- [ ] Rash Guard
- [ ] Ding Repair
- [ ] Sunblock and Zinc
- [ ] Sunglasses
- [ ] Hat
- [ ] Beach Towel and/or Sarong
- [ ] Bug Spray (with Deet)
- [ ] Flashlight and/or Petzel Headlamp
- [ ] CD's/MP3 player
- [ ] Light long pants for night (mosquito protection)
- [ ] Light long sleeve shirt for night (same)
- [ ] Camera
- [ ] Benadryl and Epipen (if you are allergic to anything)
- [ ] New Surf Mags
- [ ] Basic First Aid (Bandaids, gauze, aspirin, Neosporin, Immodium AD, etc.)
- [ ] Toothpaste, Toothbrush
- [ ] Shampoo, Conditioner, Soap
- [ ] Dry Bags for electronics (in the rainy season)
- [ ] Photocopies of important documents
- [ ] Rain Jacket (in the rainy season)
- [ ] Mosquito Net (if camping)

Renting a Car

Generally the most flexible way to travel, but if you don't think you'll ever spontaneously head to a remote surf break you just heard about over breakfast then you may not need the flexibility. Some of the advantages and disadvantages of renting a vehicle in Costa Rica are below:

Advantages of Driving

Convenience
Outside of San José a private vehicle can be very convenient. In San José, you may find that parking and traffic jams make having a car more of a headache than it is worth.

Versatility & Flexibility
If the bed and breakfast you were planning on staying in misplaces your reservation, you can hop in your car and go few miles down the road, confident that in a short time you will run across another place to stay.

If you are traveling by bus, then once you get to your destination you will probably be on foot, and a few miles down the road is a long way to walk, especially if you have lots of boards.

Speed and Efficiency
When traffic is light and the roads are good, a car can be a quick way to get around, but don't think you are going to average 60 MPH. The roads are narrow, and many wind steeply through volcanic valleys. At times you will end up stuck behind a cattle truck going five miles an hour down the center line for an hour or more.

The rain is tough on the roads and construction and repair will also often delay you. On a few occasions, we were stuck behind long lines of cars on our bicycles, much to the frustration of the drivers.

Cost
A rental car costs a lot if you're on your own, but for a group of three or four who want to visit a lot of locations it can compare favorably with the price of the bus. For example, an inexpensive four-passenger sedan can be had for $US 270 a week (including unlimited free mileage, taxes and mandatory Collision and Damage Waiver insurance).

Cost Example
Travel to Santa Rosa, a couple of beaches on the Nicoya peninsula, Chirripó, and Corcovado by public bus (there are also private buses that are about 5 times more expensive) would cost about $US 189 for three, $US 252 for four. Add in a 7 km walk from where the bus drops you to the trailheads in Santa Rosa, $US 20 or so for taxis from the bus station to a hotel when you're too exhausted to hoof it, another $US 12 to 40 for airport transfers, and getting up at 4:30 a.m. to catch the bus from San Isidro to Chirripó Park, and spending that extra few bucks seems like a good idea.

Disadvantages of Driving

Cost
As noted under advantages, a rental car can be budget friendly transportation if you're travelling with a group. However with only one or two people, you'll pay more for the convenience. A four-wheel-drive sport utility vehicle isn't absolutely necessary, but there are many places you can't get without one, and they survive the battering of the huge potholes on the paved roads

TRANSPORTATION: GETTING AROUND

much better.
A small SUV costs around $US 50 per day, plus gas (¢600 per liter or ~$US 4.60 per gallon in mid 2006) and insurance ($US 18 per day), plus a 12% airport concourse fee if you pick it up there. Don't forget that you will be paying for the car every day, so three days of hanging out on a beach will cost you at least $US 200 for your parked car. One way rentals are possible but surcharges for drop-off at your destination tend to be expensive.

Inconvenience
On the tourist trail theft from parked cars is epidemic. You must remove everything each time you stop, leave someone with the car constantly, or hire someone to watch it. It is ill advised to park even an empty car outside a secure lot overnight.

Getting lost can be an adventure or an inconvenience. You won't really be sure until you try it, but pilots and bus conductors rarely lose their way.

There are places like Tortuguero that you can't access by road even if you shell out $300 a day for a Humvee, and other places where folks without a car have fun options like a boat ride across Lake Arenal then Horseback to Monteverde.

Insulation
A car insulates you from the people, culture and wilderness. You won't meet people along the way, and it's unlikely that you'll notice the column of leaf cutter ants marching alongside the road.

Companies:

Budget is good and cheap (Book on

Driving in Costa Rica
Photo: Marco Lilliu

TRANSPORTATION: GETTING AROUND

Costa Rica by Bus

Tourist Minibuses

These buses tend to be slightly faster (half an hour on a four hour trip), more convenient (door-to-door service to major hotels) and more comfortable (all promise A/C and some deliver) than the public buses. The biggest advantage is the direct routes on segments frequented by tourists where the public buses require going out of your way or changing buses frequently. Service frequency is increasing, but on many routes there is still only a single departure each morning. Prices range from $25 to $50 pp. (5 to 10 times the public bus fares).

www.graylinecostarica.com
www.interbusonline.com

Public Buses

Far and away the cheapest mode of transportation in Costa Rica ranging in price from around $0.10 to $10.00 and often the fastest and most convenient. Buses on the main routes are modern and comfortable but typically not air-conditioned.

Although they may not be currently, these two website should give you a good idea of what's out there:

http://www.monteverdeinfo.com/costa-rica/bus-schedule.htm

http://costa-rica-guide.com/BusSchedule.html

Costa Offshore Surf
Photo: Tony Roberts

TRANSPORTATION: GETTING AROUND

In-Country Flights

Costa Rica has two domestic airlines (see schedules and rates NatureAir at www.natureair.com/, SANSA at www.flysansa.com/) that operate from two different airports near San José. The direct flights shown on the route map below last between 15 minutes and an hour, and cost between $40 and $90 each way plus taxes & fees.

Both airlines serve essentially the same outlying destinations. While nearly all flights still begin or end at San José in 2005 NatureAir started adding a few flights from Quepos and Tamarindo directly to other popular destinations and rearranged their schedule to make one stop flights from Arenal more convenient.

Tips for Travel on Domestic Airlines

Keep your camera with you. Don't pack your camera away, the views are spectacular. In fact it would be easy to forget that you are flying for transportation and not on a sightseeing trip.

Leave some extra time. These are small airlines, they don't have the highest airspace priority in San José where all their flights originate, and heavy weather can be a factor.

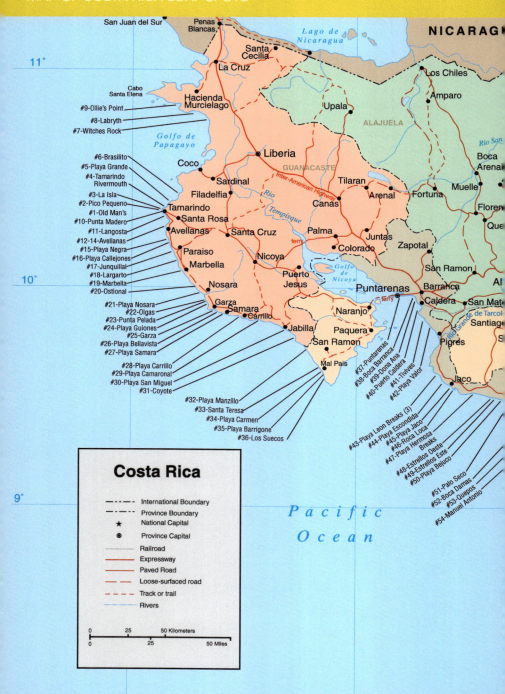

NORTH PACIFIC REGION: NICA BORDER TO MAL PAIS

Looking North to Playa Grande from Tamarindo
Photo: John Lyman

Tamarindo

Located 69 kilometers southwest of Liberia, Tamarindo is the largest North Pacific beach/surf town in the area. Great surf, beautiful coastline and a pumping nightlife are some of the attractions of this full-fledged resort. This place is extremely touristy, but its a good spot to start a surf trip in Costa. There's lots of surf shops and other stores here to pick up any missing supplies you might need. There are also car rental places here as well.

However, one can't help but feel like the town is now being run by foreigners, much to the consternation of the locals. So if a local doesn't say "hola" back, don't take it personally. You would probably do the same if your home town was invaded too. However all in all, everyone is pretty friendly.

While the surf at Playa Tamarindo is usually only good for beginners or others who are just getting back into the groove, there are some great spots to surf around Tamarindo.

To the north is Playa Grande (#5) and to the south is Playa Langosta (#11), Playa Avellanas (#12-#14) and Playa Negra (#15). Theses breaks are described below. Also as mentioned above, boats can be chartered here for trips to Witches Rock (#7) and Ollie's Point (#9).

Finding a Board & Gear in Tamarindo

There is at least 6 surf shops so it won't be a problem to find a board to either buy or rent or other gear.

Make sure to shop around and to bar ter the price down a bit. Usually if you offer to pay cash, they will lower the pirce even more by 10% or so.

Also make sure to ask if fins are included as they are quite expensive here. Also ask for a deal if you buy a leash and a board bag at the same time.

We also recommend purchasing a rash guard if you don't have one. For 20 bucks your skin will thank you forever. Trust me, I've had way too many moles removed by scalpel due to surfing without a rashguard when I was younger.

#1 – Tamarindo Beach Break

This is the beach break right in front of the town. It's really only suitable for beginners when there's a decent swell coming in and the other breaks in the area are too big.

#2 – Pico Pequeño

Pico Pequeño a rocky point in front of the hotel Tamarindo. It can get barrelling at times. Best conditions at a mid tide. Pequeño is located south of Tamarindo's rivermouth.

#3 – La Isla

Also called Isla Capitan. This is the island right in front of Tamarindo. It can turn into a big wave spot when southern swells are big enough. ONLY FOR ADVANCED SURFERS. LOTS OF ROCKS AND URCHINS.

NORTH PACIFIC REGION: TAMARINDO

#4 – Tamarindo Rivermouth

Also simply called "El Estero" in Spanish, meaning "the estuary." Dont confue this place with the other estuary/rivermouth near Tamarindo, at Playa Langosta.

Solid right beachbreak with hollow waves as they hit the inside reef. Best conditions are west swells with offshore winds. at mid-high tide. Known as a classic longboard wave with a sweet shoulder offering high, noseriding lefts & rights. It can get a little packed here, but Playa Grande is just north, so go there if there's too many people on the peak.

Getting to Tamarindo

From San Jose or Liberia
If you are coming from San Jose on the Panamerican Highway #1 north, you will reach Liberia. At the main intersection turn left and follow the signs to Flamingo, Conchal, & Tamarindo. In this road just to follow the signs that will lead you to these beautiful beaches. After passing Filadelfia and Belen look for the road signs to Tamarindo, Flamingo, Conchal, Sugar Beach, Potrero, Avellanas and Langosta.

From Nosara / Samara / Carrillo & From Tambor / Montezuma / Mal País / Santa Teresa

If you are coming from all these places take the road to Nicoya and continue to Santa Cruz. There are two ways to reach Tamarindo:

1- After Santa Cruz look for the road sign to Tamarindo Beach. Continue the road which turns into a gravel road and just follow the signs to Tamarindo.

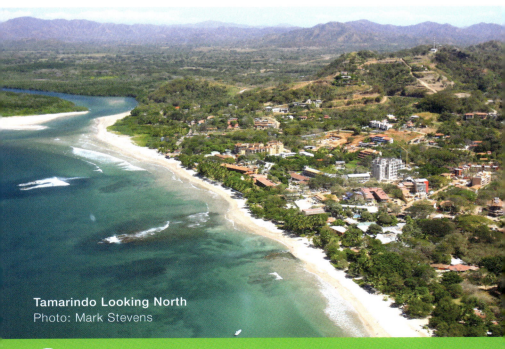

Tamarindo Looking North
Photo: Mark Stevens

NORTH PACIFIC REGION: NORTH OF TAMARINDO

2- After Santa Cruz follow the main road towards Belen. Once in Belen follow the signs to Tamarindo.

Places to Stay around Tamarindo

CALA LUNA Hotel & Villas
Secluded at the southern end of Tamarindo and Playa Langosta. This enchanting hotel offers 21 luxury villas and 20 deluxe hotel rooms and by far stands in a class of its own. We were lucky enough to stay here for a couple nights. It's absolutely spectacular. www.calaluna.com

Your Hotel
Consectetuer adipiscing elit. Etiam luctus, nibh eu euismod facilisis, augue nunc interdum diam, et iaculis sapien eros non erat.
www.your-hotel.com

Your Hotel
Consectetuer adipiscing elit. Etiam luctus, nibh eu euismod facilisis, augue nunc interdum diam, et iaculis sapien eros non erat.
www.your-hotel.com

Surfing North of Tamarindo

#5 – Playa Grande

Playa Grande Beach break, located about 20 minutes north of Tamarindo. Accessible by road. Playa Grande is a good option for those looking to avoid the crowds often found in Tamarindo and surf world class waves right out their front door. Grande offers one of the area's most consistent waves and there are several private house rentals located right on the beach.

This offers surfers a more remote option than Tamarindo while still offering easy access (15 minute drive) to the amenities of the town. Grande has very few services such as restuarants, shops,etc, however, all house rentals are equipped with full kitchens. For rentals, check out www.surf-costarica.com.

Directions: To get to Playa Grande from Tamarindo, drive norht along the main road that goes parallel to the beach, then take a left at the main intersection (there's a sign for Playa Grande). Then take another left at the cross road (again, there's another sign).

At the first left, if you need gasoline, go right instead of left and you will see a gas station on the left about 10 minutes down the road. The gas station does not appear on any of the recent maps for some reason.

There's also a cafe called "Cafe Cafe" on the road going out from Tamarindo, which rocks.

For Parking at Grande, park in the Parking Lot and pay the dude a couple dollars to watch your car, its worth the money as the area is known for thefts.

Places to Stay around Playa Grande

Your Hotel
Consectetuer adipiscing elit. Etiam luctus, nibh eu euismod facilisis, augue nunc interdum diam, et iaculis sapien eros non erat.
www.your-hotel.com

Your Hotel
Consectetuer adipiscing elit. Etiam luctus, nibh eu euismod facilisis, augue

NORTH PACIFIC REGION: NORTH OF TAMARINDO

nunc interdum diam, et iaculis sapien eros non erat.
www.your-hotel.com

#6 – Brasilito

Brasilito is fickle and doesn't break that well so we only recommend it for beginners. It's a $25 taxi ride from Tamarindo. No direct public bus.

Brasilito, a small fishing village with a few restaurants and cabins, is located 45 kms from the town of Santa Cruz or 70 kms. from Liberia. The beach attracts more locals than tourists and has a moderate selection of budget and mid-range hotels.

To get there, take the route Liberia- Guardia- Filadelfia- Belén- Huacas- Playa Brasilito.

Besides a few hotels, there are bars and restaurants as well as an internet cafe in town. Here one can also find a number of rental shops for surf gear, horses, dive equipment, motorbikes and much more.

Places to Stay around Brasilito

Hotel Brasilito features ocean views, palm tree gardens, an outdoor restaurant and cooling sea breezes. In addition they offer free wireless internet. Their staff speak English, German and Spanish and are able to help you with any information you may need. Contact them at hotel@brasilito.com or at 506-

Locked in at Playa Grande
Photo: John L. Lyman
Surfer: Unknown

NORTH PACIFIC REGION: NORTH OF TAMARINDO

Ollie's Point
Photo: Alfonso Petrirena

Witches Rock
Photo: Alfonso Petrirena
Surfer: Gustavo Mora

NORTH PACIFIC REGION: NORTH OF TAMARINDO

2-654-4237 or www.brasilito.com/

#7 – Witch's Rock (Boat Access Only)

Witch's Rock or Roca Bruja in spanish is on Playa Naranjo. It's one of the best breaks in the country. This wilderness point break is located in the national park of Santa Rosa.

The wave is accessible by a 4wd vehicle for most of the year, with sparse camping - bring your own water and bug repellent. Lots of boats come in, make sure they are licensed to enter the park. The waves are clean, with lots of offshore winds especially from December to April. Picks up swells from the SSW and SW and can throw barrels. Best wave size is chest high to two feet overhead, any bigger and it tends to close out.

This super-fun beach break on Playa Naranjo gets its name from the huge monthic rock in front, which in turn gets its name from the noises you can hear from its huge crevasses. The main break is between the rock and the rivermouth (watch out for crocodiles near the river estuary). There are also rocks around the rivermouth to watch out for. The 2 mile stretch of beach with hollow sand bottom beach breaks creating long lefts and rights. Take off can be steep, however offshores generally keep the wave open and easy to surf. Best conditions with a west/southwest swell at incoming to high tide.

Directions: There's two options. The easy one is to hire a boat from Playa del Coco or Tamarindo. The harder one is to drive. From San Jose, take the Interamerican highway to Liberia. Continue on the Interamerican highway past Liberia Guanacaste about 20 miles to Potrerillos. The entrance to Santa Rosa Sector is on the left, six miles past Potrerillos. Playa Naranjo (where Witches Rock is located) is reached by an 8 mile stretch of dirt road from the Santa Rosa Station (La Casona, the big wooden house). This road is only accessible during dry season with 4WD.

#8 – Labyrinth (Boat Access Only)

Labyrinth or Labyrintos in spanish is a difficult right hander that breaks at lower tides when the rocks are exposed. It can throw a mean barrel and produce a workable shoulder for about 60 yards before it pounds shut on the rocks. Boat access only, make sure your captain is permitted to enter the Santa Rosa National Park. It's close to Ollies Point (#9).

Do not charge this wave unless you have a lot of experience. There is no beach just cliffs and rocks, you can only go right, if you go left you will en up in rocks. You do not want to get caught in the inside either. If you do you need to, paddle to the right, otherwise you will end up in a big pinball machine with large jagged rocks and no where to go. This wave peels perfectly right with a fast steep take off and a big tube behind it. The reef is really shallow If your not very accurate with your turns you need to pull out preety quick. On the inside the boulders start to expose, and you need to solum throuh them. Its a Hairy dangerous wave but a hell of a ride.

NORTH PACIFIC REGION: NORTH OF TAMARINDO

#9 – Ollie's Point (Boat Access Only)

Ollie's Point is also called Potrero Grande by the locals. Right point at the rivermouth with fast, hollow waves that roll on the beach endlessly breaking over a rocky bottom. Ollie's Point was one of the waves surfing in Endless Summer 2.

The take off is at a series of rocks with slow entry. Best conditions are an outgoing to mid low tide and south/southwest swells. One of the only problems with Ollie's is that it requires a good south swell to get going. Witch's Rock, Playa Grande, and Playa Avellanas are typically bigger.

The spot is named after Oliver North, who was a CIA agent at the time. The area was used for the United States' covert war again the Sandinistas, the current government of Nicaragua at the time.

In the Murcielago section of Santa Rosa National Park, amidst rocky peaks and valleys, you can walk around the old CIA training camp, as well as a house that belonged to the former Nicaraguan dictator Somoza, who held power until the Sandinista's took over.

Accessing Ollie's Point: Hire a boat from Playa del Coco or Tamarindo.

Secret Spot

There's also a wave north of Witch's Rock (South of Ollies and Labryths), but we're not going to give it away. However, if you ask your boat captain nicely, they may take you there if the conditions are right.

Where to Stay around Witch's Rock and Ollies Point

Witch's Rock has a camping area at Naranjo Beach which is open 24 hours and provides picnic tables and charcoal cookstoves. Restrooms and showers are available, but no potable water.

There is no camping allowed near Ollie's Point.

Most people who surf Ollie's or Witch's usually stay either in Playa Los Cocos or Tamarindo.

Playas del Coco near the Gulf of Papagayo is the town with the largest infrastructure in this area. Besides shops, restaurants, casinos and markets, you'll find all kind of hotels and cabins from simple to deluxe. The Playas del Coco Beach is easy accessible from Liberia - Sardinal - Playas del Coco (35 km).

Cocos isn't a surf beach, it is a port, which makes it very popular with divers and fishermen, who ship out from its anchorages, and surfers bound for Witch's Rock and Ollie's.

Recommended Boat Companies

Your Surf Camp/Boat Company
Consectetuer adipiscing elit. Etiam luctus, nibh eu euismod facilisis, augue nunc interdum diam, et iaculis sapien eros non erat. Quisque semper turpis sed nunc porttitor viverra. Sed lorem leo, vehicula
www.surfcamp.com

Your Surf Camp/Boat Company
Consectetuer adipiscing elit. Etiam luctus, nibh eu euismod facilisis, augue

NORTH PACIFIC REGION: SOUTH OF TAMARINDO

nunc interdum diam, et iaculis sapien eros non erat. Quisque semper turpis

#10 – Punta Madero

Located on the long point just south of Tamarindo. From the beach in beach in Tamarindo, it's the first point to your left if your facing the ocean. The point needs a decent south west swell to really get going, but when it does, watch out! It's a great wave but it breaks on a rock reef so 'ten cuidado' (be careful).

#11 – Langosta Reefs and Estuary

A right and left point break that curls off the mouth of a a small river, located 1 km south of Tamarindo.

You will notice depending on the tide tha tthe wave peaks at the same place every time. Even though this is a river mouth there is a coral head that is exposed during low tide and remains just below the surface at high tide. Also keep an eye on your position with regard to the shore. (To the north of the mouth are submerged rocks that extend from the beach out fairly far)
It can be as much fun as Playa Negra on fair sized surf. One of the better spots in the immediate area.

To Access: InTamarindo there is a dirt road that runs past Cala Luna Resort. Keep going south on this road for about 1-2km. Area was being developed with apartment buildings overlooking the break last time we was there. Ask any locals and they'll point you in the right direction if you get lost.

From Costa to Nicaragua

If you have time, checking out southern Nicaragua (or more) can yield a treasure trove of good surf. Nicaragua's most popular surfing region, San Juan del Surf, is easily accessible from northern Costa Rica. You can get to San Juan del Sur from Tamarindo in under 7 hours on a good day.

Border Crossing between Costa Rica & Nicaragua

The border crossing at Peñas Blancas is very busy and delays are frequent, especially during the holidays (Christmas and Easter). Please keep this in mind as you make your travel plans and strive for patience. You will be in a beautiful and relaxing place very soon! The border crossing is open daily between 6:00 a.m. and 8:00 p.m.

Rental Cars & Inter-country Bus Transportation

Rental cars are generally not allowed to cross the border between countries. It is best to contact your rental car company first to double check their policy - a good one to try is Alamo at www.alamocostarica.com. To travel from Liberia, Costa Rica to San Juan del Sur, you may wish to take a taxi to the border and arrange transportation with your hotel in Nicaragua. Or, the Tica Bus (www.ticabus.com) and Nica Bus (www.nicabus.com) make stops in Liberia and Rivas (Rivas is approximately 30 minutes from San Juan del Sur), and you can take an inexpensive taxi ride from Rivas to San Juan del Sur.

Immigration & Customs

Tourists and Costa Rican citizens do not have to pay any fees upon leaving Costa Rica; however foreign residents living in Costa Rica must pay a $20 departure tax. North American and most European countries are not required to have a visa to enter Nicaragua, but they will need a passport that does not expire within six months, and a small entry fee is required ($10) when arriving at the Managua International Airport. Costa Rican residents or nationals must have a visa to enter Nicaragua, which can be obtained at the Nicaraguan Consulate of the country of residency, and by paying a $25 fee.

Make sure to check out our **Blue Planet Nicaragua Surfing Guide** for details on where to surf in Nicaragua:

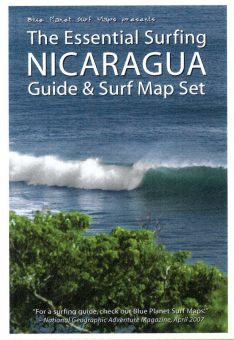

NORTH PACIFIC REGION: SOUTH OF TAMARINDO (AVELLANAS)

The waves break over a rocky shelf, with more sandy stretches to the south of the rivermouth. Watch for the boils at lower tides to find a hollow peak. Best size is chest high to 3 feet overhead, when it's bigger can close out. The main break is behind the Barcelo Langosta, but they have made it nearly impossible to park near there. You'll find a few spots to park about 200 meters north. The rights during a swell with a lot of west in it can go for over 200 meters. The crowds are a bit lighter here due to the poor access, but the Barcelo guests think they own the peak, and the locals don't give up many waves.

El Sapo (the toad) sometime is also here in the lava formed reefs between Madero Point and the Langosta Beach estuary. Look for the big rock that looks like a toad or frog and you've found it. If you're not too sure about surfing over sharp rock reefs, try coming here at low tide first to check it out, or surf some of the local break breaks instead.

Surfing Playa Avellanas and Playa Negra

Located 15 kilometers south of Tamarindo, these laid-back beaches are favored by surfers for their consistent waves. Avellanas' prevailing reef break, dubbed "Little Hawaii", can be a challenge for even seasoned surfers. South of Avellenas' white sand beach is Playa Negra, a darker beach dominated by a rocky coastline. Negra is famous for its reef point breaks and excellent barrels. Visitors can anticipate steady breezes and ideal surfing conditions between the months of December and April.

Both beaches are relatively undeveloped and are geared towards the surfing community. A handful of cabinas and hostels offer standard accommodations for the budget traveler. Playas Negra and Avellanas can be difficult to access during the wet season without 4WD, as dirt roads turn into mud and small rivers must be forded.

Both spots are ideal locations for surf-

NORTH PACIFIC REGION: SOUTH OF TAMARINDO (AVELLANAS)

ers looking for a more relaxing, remote surfing vacation with less nightlife and more, dawn patrol sessions.

Although most travelers opt to stay in Tamarindo and make the drive to these breaks, if you choose to stay at these locations for your surf vacation, the best way to enjoy these breaks is to stay at the respective hotel in front of the break.

To Access: Avellanas and Negra are accessed by a dirt road from Huacas (just outside of Tamarindo). Check road conditions before driving (beach and internal road available).

Best Time to Surf: December to April
For those looking for a remote vacation experience, these are the ideal destination.

#12 – Avellanas breaks ("Little Hawaii" AND the Estuary/El Estero)

Playa Avellanas, located 10 km south of Tamarindo, has 4 good surf breaks. Little Hawaii is the most northern break and the gnarliest as well.
A series of rights and lefts from a rivermouth offering a series of peaks including reefs and beach breaks. The northern end of the rivermouth boasts an outside reef break, "Little Hawaii," which works best on a west or northwest swell and is ideal for longboarders. The rivermouth is a rock bottom right that can get very hollow and best at low tide in the am.

#13 – Avellanas breaks (The Tree/El Palo)

Good beach break, but can be crowded.

#14 – Avellanas breaks (Lola's/El Parquero)

This beach break is perfect for beginners and intermediate surfers depending on the swell size. It's the least spectular break on Avellanas, but it's the most forgiving as well and it's the least

Playa Negra
Photo: Alfonso Petrirena
Surfer: Maikol Tablada

competitive/territorial as well.

To Access: The break is directly in front of the parking lot and Lola's bar which is on the right when facing the water.

#15 – Playa Negra

A right point break with very fast waves, 350 kms from San Jose. Playa Negra is one of the best breaks in the country. Located 5 km south of playa Avellanas.

12 kilometers south of Tamarindo offering a rock-reef right break that is fast & hollow at low tide creating a picture perfect ride. Best conditions in the morning with a mid tide going out. Negra will pick up swell from many directions and crowds can be a factor.

Follow the signs to Hotel Playa Negra.

You can park your car at the Hotel Playa Negra. Sit outside over by the rocks for the best peak. The wave has two distinct sections that barrel. On smaller days, there is a left, but its short and breaks over jagged rocks.

Things to Avoid
Avoid parking at the beach with any valuables in the car. The remoteness which makes this area so attractive, also makes it an easy target for petty theft while you are in the water.

Where to Stay around Avellanas and Playa Negra

CABINAS LAS OLAS
Located in Avellanes offering rustic, bungalows on a quiet property within a short walk to the surf. These are good options for budget travelers looking for basic accommodations and do not want to stay in Tamarindo.

HOTEL PLAYA NEGRA
The Hotel Playa Negra, consists of a few individual villa style cabinas spread along the beautiful beach of this area.
www.bbplayanegra.com

www.playanegra.com

www.monocongolodge.com

Playa Nega is about 1/2 mile from Los Pargos (the nearest village).

Surfing around Nosara

Nosara has become increasingly popular amongst traveling surfers as it offers a more laid back, relaxed atmosphere than its bustling neighbor to the north, Tamarindo, while boasting world class surf almost all year.

The small community of Nosara offers visitors a unique experience with a variety of moderate accommodations, activities such as surfing, fishing, horseback riding and more.

Nosara has become a popular destination for repeat visitors to Costa Rica who are looking for a different experience than Tamarindo or Hermosa. This is one of Costa Rica's most beautiful areas and the only noise that you will hear in Nosara is the sound of the waves crashing and the monkeys howling.

Getting There
Nosara is accessed by taking the fer-

NORTH PACIFIC REGION: SOUTH OF TAMARINDO (NOSARA)

ry from Tempisque Ferry across the Nicoya Peninsula and then drive for 2 hours until reaching Nosara. There is also a small airport.

#16 – Playa Callejones

Good beach break. Ask some locals and go on an adventure! We can't give everything away.

#17 – Junquillal

A beach break and a left reef that work better on higher tides. There are many peaks with hollow, fast rights and lefts. The waves jack up off the sandbar creating a tough entry. On a large enough swell, try surfing at Playa Blanca directly in front of the Iguana Azul which offers double overhead epic lefts.

Location is south of tamarindo, north of nosara, and straight west of a little town called paraiso.

WEBCAM: www.surf-costarica.com/break/junquillal.htm

A ten minute walk down the beach from Hotel Iquanazul, this break can get really fun. During higher tides, there are many peaks that offer hollow, fast

Road to Nosara, rainy season
Photo: Fred Jenkins

NORTH PACIFIC REGION: SOUTH OF TAMARINDO (NOSARA)

rights and lefts the waves jack up off the sand bar very quickly creating a tough, but exciting, drop in. It breaks very close to shore in shallow water over a sandy bottom.

Junquillal is a pretty remote area and on some days you might see two or three people on the beach and no one in the water. BEWARE when your walking out, there are sting rays. a sting can ruin a day of surf pretty easy. if traveling through dont miss this spot.

Directions to Playa Junquillal

BY CAR: From San Jose take the Pan-American Highway north towards Liberia. You can either get to the Guacamaya Lodge taking the Tempisque Bridge (4 hour drive) or the Liberia route (5 hour drive).

Bridge Route(Puente de la Amistad): After the village of Limonal is a big Shell Gas station. Turn lift here it will lead you to the bridge.

After 20-minute ride, follow the road until it dead ends and turn right towards Nicoya. Follow the signs to Santa Cruz, after the traffic light in Santa Cruz you pass a metal bridge and turn immediately to the left after the bridge. Follow the road for 18 km. You pass another metal bridge and turn left again. Approximately 200 mt after that turn there is a right turn. Follow the road until the small town of Paraiso. After the soccer place turn left and you arrive after 4 km to Playa Junquillal

Liberia route: If you decide not to take the ferry follow the signs to Liberia

Ripping it up at Guiones
Photo: John L. Lyman
Surfer: Unknown

NORTH PACIFIC REGION: MAL PAIS & SANTA TERESA

once in Liberia take the left highway at the intersection to Santa Cruz. Just before the bridge leading into Santa Cruz turn right and Follow the road for 18 km. You pass another metal bridge and turn left again. Approximately 200 mt after that turn there is a right turn. Follow the road until the small town of Paraiso. After the soccer place turn left and you arrive after 4 km to Playa Junquillal.

BY BUS: Two local bus lines leave San Jose to Santa Cruz. TRALAPA and ALFARO. They have almost and hour schedule. Fare is about $ 5 and it takes approximately 5 hours. Alfaro number is 2222 27 50 or 2223 82 29 and Tralapa number is 2221 72 02
From Santa Cruz a Taxi brings you to Guacamaya Lodge for $ 30 in 45 Minutes.

There is one Tralapa bus at 2pm who has a connection in Santa Cruz to Playa Junquillal.

#18 – Largarto

Good beach break. Ask some locals and go on an adventure! We can't give everything away.

#19 – Marbella

Located between Junquillal and Ostional, this is one of the area's most consistent breaks offering excellent conditions with the presence of offshore winds. There are no services in the area. Most people either drive through or stay in Nosara or Playa Junquillal.

Marbella the town is about 1/2 mile east of the break. Marbella has a few small grocery stores and a few restaurants. Locals call them "sodas" in Costa Rica. Marbella is about an hour south of Negra, but it could take dramatically more time depending on the rain and mud.

There's a campground on the beach.

#20 – Ostional

Beach and reef break with rights and lefts that works on higher tides and south to southwest swells. Located north of Nosara.

Ostional is a little village north of Nosara. From San Jose, there are direct buses to Nosara. Ostional during the rainy season only by 4wd accessible.

There are two ways to get to Ostional. One is to drive along the coast from Playa Negra, Marbella, etc. This route is only recommended in the dry season and with a 4x4. The other routh is from Nicoya which is inland, then to Nosara, then head north to El Ostional. A 4x4 for the last leg is still recommended.

#21 – Playa Nosara

Nosara the town is about 3 miles (5km) inland from Playa Nosara, Playa Guiones and the coast in general.

Decent beach break with peaks and shallow rock reef lefts that get barrelling with a large south or southwest swell. Nosara Beach break, with lefts and rights. About 350 kms from San

NORTH PACIFIC REGION: NOSARA & SAMARA

Jose. You go from San Jose to Nicoya and from there to Nosara. It takes approx. 5 hours to get there.

Check out www.surf-costarica.com/dailyphoto/nosara.html

The best surf break is down the beach some in front of a huge, lone Palm Tree. You'll know by all the surfers in the water out in front of it. This place is a smorgishboard of kneeboarders, longboarders, beginners, groms and ocean goers of all sorts. HOWEVER you can easily paddle down the beach and find an uncrowded peak for yourself.

It's a fun wave, thats much more forgiving than nearby waves. Even on big days. Its breaks on almost all tides (though it favors higher tides) and during the winter months, offshores are plentiful.

#22 – Olgas

On Playa Pelada beach near the town of Nosara, in front of the restaurant with the same name.

Olgas a very nice beach with a variety of waves. very consistent with warm water all year. If you are in this part of Costa Rica, dont miss it. Playa Pelada is a laid back spot. We have a sunset every night. Don't worry about the fire nobody cares. Turn up the music. I catch a lobster whenever I get the urge for one. The fishing is incredible. The diving is good. Nightlife close by and there is surf every day. The crowds are just enough people in the water to make it fun. Check it out on www.aventurapelada.com

#23 – Punta Pelada

A rock reef on the north side which is best with a north swell at incoming high tide. Not very consistent and gets very crowded .

North of Playa Guiones and south of Playa Nosara, Punta Pelada is easily accessible by car and then a short walk.

Park your car front of the beach under the trees. you can eat and drink at la Luna (south of beach) or at Olga's in front of the surf. Also you will see Hotel Nosara from the line up.

The rock reef on the north side is best with a north swell at incoming high tide. Its not very consistent and gets very crowded.

#24 – Playa Guiones

A beach break with a left point that works better at high tides and early in the morning. This area offers some of the most consistent year-round surf ranging from head-high to double overhead and much less crowded than the Tamarindo area.

To Access: A mile or so south of Nosara. just turn toward the beach at the Cafe de Paris. It's then about 1/2 mile to beach.

#25 – Garza

Good beach break. Ask some locals and go on an adventure! We can't give everything away.

NORTH PACIFIC REGION: MAL PAIS & SANTA TERESA

#26 – Playa Bellavista

Good beach break. Ask some locals and go on an adventure! We can't give everything away.

Places to Stay around Nosara & Samara

The small community of Nosara offers visitors a unique experience with a variety of moderate accommodations.

HARBOR REEF LODGE
Located only 2 minutes walking distance from Playa Guiones. This Lodge is surrounded by jungle and gardens, and offers suites, cabinas and rooms which are all extremely comfortable and quaint with plenty of privacy and seclusion.

CASA SERENITY
Just what the names says. Pretty peaceful, a small place with fairly spacious rooms. Call for details.

CASA PACIFICA
A two-bedroom, two bath house that is about 200 meters away from the shoreline. The house can accommodate up to 6 people comfortably. Call for details.

VILLA TAYPE
Just minutes from the beautiful beach of Playa Guiones. It's a small hotel, with seclusion and jungle. Swimming pool.

Others:
blewdogs.com
safarisurfschool.com
cafedeparis.net
harborreef.com
refugiodelsol.com

pacho's resort
nosarabeachhotel.com

#27 – Playa Samara

Playa Samara is usually a small beginner beach-break with rights and lefts. Samara is directly south by paved road from Nicoya or Nosara.

The best waves are about a 1/4 mile from the town center in front of Bar Las Olas. Island and reef surfing are available by boat for more experienced surfers. Playa Samara is a beginner/intermediate, longboard surfbreak. This is unusual in Costa Rica where heavy waves are the norm. Big waves hit the outside on the reef or the island though.

Samara is a lot of fun. For the serious surfer there are boat trips to excellent waves in the Samara bay and at nearby beaches, notably Camaronal.

For general info check: www.samara-beach.com

#28 – Playa Carrillo

Good beach break. Ask some locals and go on an adventure! We can't give everything away.

#29 – Playa Camaronal

Located down between Nosara and Mal Pais. Nice beach break that is surrounded by rocks. This break is very consistent and offers surf year-round Best conditions from the south, or southwest.

NORTH PACIFIC REGION: MAL PAIS & SANTA TERESA

Surfing Mal Pais & Santa Teresa

Mal País, located on the southern tip of the Nicoya Peninsula, is another rising, yet still fairly untouched, surf destination in Costa Rica. Mal Pais/Santa Teresa is a very small community scattered along the pale, gold beaches with a beautiful backdrop of green vegetation.

This area is ideal for surfers looking for a remote surfing experience with no nightlife, just good, consistent waves and a great atmosphere. Most waves in the area are best for intermediate surfers, however a large swell will put the area's more fickle reef breaks in epic form for advanced surfers.

Getting There
Mal País is accessed by taking a ferry from Puntarenas and then driving about 1 hour on mostly paved road into town.

Advice: In this area, you will find many upaved roads that are easy to drive during the dry season (November to May), but please note that during the rainy season (May to November) a 4x4 is highly recommended.

Best Surf Time: December to April

#30 – Playa San Miguel

Also check out the beaches between Playa Camaronal and Mal Pais. Venture

Santa Theresa Sunset
Photo: Thornton Cohen (www.nomadpics.com)

of the beaten path. Make sure you trust your 4X4, there's at least a couple rivers to cross.

For instance, December thorough April, go through Samara, then Carrillo. Past Carrillo take the Punta Islita turnoff (don't miss it) and cross the river, best at low tide. Go about a mile until you see the ocean on your right over a cow pasture. Open the wooden gate and drive to beach. In the rainy season the river is usually too high to cross. Try at low tide or go by boat from Samara.

Nothing here but surf. This beach is yet to be developed and there are no services near. It's worth the trip however. Samara is only 20 minutes by boat or car and it has everything, good bars, restaurants, hotels, boats for camaronal available. Camaronal is almost always good and sometimes great. Holds up to triple overhead. Surfable all day. Sometimes wind or strong currents can make it bad. Rarely there is no swell at all.

This area is ideal for surfers looking for a remote surfing experience with no nightlife, just good, consistent waves and a great atmosphere.

#31 – Playa Coyote

About 3 miles north of Santa Teresa take the dirt road that veers left to the beach. You'll see a rocky point straight ahead that turns into a good point break when it's big. Park your 4x4 on the beach and hit the surf. There's a good area to camp about 25 yards to your left near the trees.

There's a rip by the rocky point that takes you out. Surf the rights there or head 50 yards south for the best left peak. Lots of lefts and rights across the beach.

Also called Jackals.

Check out www.playacoyote.com

#32 – Playa Mazanillo

There's some great beach breaks on the north end of the bay.

#33 – Santa Teresa

Good lefts and rights at this hollow beach break. Santa Teresa can get quite crowded though since it's so accessible. Tends to pick up more swell than nearby breaks and holds shape better at low tide. Take a right at the crossroads and continue 3km. Best conditions on west/southwest swell.

North of Mal Pais by 2 miles look for sign on cabinas with the name Santa Teresa spelled something like that. Then head for the beach.

A cool place to stay is Zeneida's cabinas, very cheap and just in front of Santa Teresa's spot. There's also a surf camp in Mal Pais but Santa Teresa is better. When you arrive at the end of the road, Mal Pais is on the left and Santa Teresa is on the right.

#34 – Playa Carmen

A beach break that peaks with some rock reef. This wave offers a long right wall and a shorter left breaking over

NORTH PACIFIC REGION: MAL PAIS & SANTA TERESA

a sloping sand bottom. When these breaks get big, try the nearby reef breaks in Manzanillo or to the south of Carmen. Best conditions on west/southwest swell.

Playa Carmen is about 3/4 of a mile south of Santa Teresa and about 1 mile north of Mal Pais.

#35 – Playa Barrigone

Also called Barrigone Point or more commonly the Mar Azul Point Break, a left hand point break. It breaks on a reef and can be pretty consistent, especially on south swells and mid to low tide. It's basically in front of the Mar Azul restaurant.

#36 – Los Suecos

Good beach break. Ask some locals and go on an adventure! We can't give everything away.

Places to Stay around Mal Pais & Santa Teresa

It's a very small community scattered along the pale, gold beaches with a beautiful backdrop of green vegetation. Very few services are available, though the accommodations are choice.

TROPICO LATINO

Tropico Latino Lodge is located directly on the beach at Santa Teresa de Malpais. There are six spacious comfortably furnished bungalows, each with a big porch and hammock.

THE PLACE

The spacious bungalows are surrounded by a lush tropical garden with water ponds and outside showers. Each room has a different theme, shape and accent. Great drinks and a restaurant (damn good steaks.)

HOTEL FLOR BLANCA

Honeymoon paradise…in our opinion, one of Costa Rica's finest getaways. There are ten villas (three of which are two bedroom, two stories) set in gardens fashioned from the tropical forest, accessed by winding pathways of soft-edged flat pebbles.

HOTEL MILAREPA

Located on the northern end of Santa Teresa and directly on the beach with completely unique bungalows. Pretty romantic place, too. If you're a surfer couple, stay here.

THE MARCH HOUSE

One word: luxury. March House has the most spacious and comfortable accommodations in Mal Pais. Just one house, and a sanctuary for docile relaxation and meditation. It's also big bucks - if you're like some corporate exec that digs surfing, this is probably the place for you.

ranchos-itanna.com

tranquilobackpackers.com

zencostarica.com

surfing-malpais.com

malpaissurfcamp.com

theplacemalpais.com

moanslodge.com

NORTH PACIFIC REGION: MAL PAIS & SANTA TERESA

sunsetreefhotel.com

bungalows-vistadeolas.com

lahaciendademalpais.com

PHOTOGRAPHY:

artstarproductions.com
orlysurfphoto.com

CENTRAL PACIFIC REGION

Looking South toward Playa Hermosa
Photo: Marco Lilliu

Surfing in Playa Hermosa / Jaco

Playa Hermosa and nearby Jaco is THE definitive surf mecca of the central pacific coast. This area arguably offers the most consistent year-round surf with over 3 ½ miles of steep beaches with excellent exposure to swells from almost any direction. Although this area is extremely popular, there are so many peaks up an down the beach that you are likely to find an uncrowded, head high peak at almost any time of year.

Playa Hermosa is a small community of surfer friendly hotels and small restaurants & all accommodations are located beachfront with surf right out the door. Because the surf in Playa Hermosa is more challenging than nearby Jaco, this area attracts a more experienced surfer.

Playa Jaco, located just 2 short hours from the international airport, has become one of Costa Rica's most visited beach towns, especially amongst the traveling surf community. Jaco is a small, yet extremely active town geared towards surfers, parties & nightlife. As you walk down the "strip," you will find countless surf shops, restaurants, bars, discos and a variety of accommodations. Hermosa is geared more towards the hard-core surfer while Jaco is designed for the active type looking for plenty of hotels, surf shops, bars, discos and an overwhelming nightlife.

Getting There

One of Hermosa's greatest advantages: located just 2 hours on paved road from the international airport in San José.

Jaco looking North
Photo: Fred Jenkins

CENTRAL PACIFIC REGION: PUNTARENAS BREAKS

Best Surf Time: May to November

#37 – Puntarenas

Good beach break. Ask some locals and go on an adventure! We can't give everything away.

#38 – Boca Barranca

A river mouth with a very long left, located 100 kms of San Jose with excellent access, paved road. Many places to stay. Dark water during rainy season scares off many. Boca Barranca and any other nearby beach are no contaminated. Boca Barranca offers some of the best waves of the country.

A very long left that breaks off a rivermouth. This is an ideal wave for longboarding as it does not get hollow, however on a good day, rides are up to 500yds. Best on south or southwest swell & dawn patrol. Water can be extremely dirty after a rain so be prepared!

Accesss: Located a 45 min. drive north of the hotel, Boca Barranca. Follow signs to Puerto Caldera/ Puntarenas. An extremely long left in front of a river mouth which can go for up to 500 yard. Not very hollow, ideal for long boards. Paddle out to the north of the river mouth. Breaks over sand and small river rocks. The ride of your life. River mouth can get dirty after a rain. Protect all open cuts, bring alcohol to clean out ears after surfing. Pay to park your car in the lot on the point. Perfect wave for longboarding.

Tides: Best around a dead low tide incoming.
Swell: Best in a due south/southwest swell. Perro Fino is a good indicator.

ACCESS: Just take a bus or drive to Jaco, then to Puntarenas, ask and the locals will tell you where the break is. Upon arriving into Boca Baranca, you'll cross a bridge, this is where you want to get off, as the break is at the rivermouth, the wave breaks for what seems like a mile. it's worth the bus trip. well worth the bus trip if you enjoy left handers. Be careful at low tide, as the bottom is a mixture of really sharp rocks and sand. Also, be cautious as crocodiles have been known to frequent the rivermouth.

Just North of Puerto Caldera look for the bridge over Rio Barranca.

Take first left and double back next to bridge drive to the end and pay the old guy behind the fence 1000 colones to park. Other parking is avail. but expect your car to be broken into. High theft area. River runoff makes water
brown but not as polluted as it used to be. When on, 800 yard waves are possible. Watch out for crocs in the river they've been known to swim out to the lineup!

Some lodging available in guest houses just north of the big resort
(way over priced). Take the road to the resort (left branch on main hwy) and drive past. Gated houses on the left rent cabinas.

Super fun looooooooong lefts. Some sections quicker than others, but all very makeable.
Pretty mellow hot dog or longboard wave. Usually, a friendly vibe in the water but can get real crowded when

good as it's the closet break to San Jose and world class when on.

Stop there on every trip to Costa to check it out. It needs a big south swell to work, but when its going off (sadly quite rare...), one of the best places to be! (WANNASURF)

#39 –Dona Ana

Ultra-crowded, left point break

Dona ana is the break to the direct NE of boca barranca, it is very fast and sometimes hollow at low tide it works all the way up untill high tide. On huge S swell this break will link up with boca creating very very very long lefts.

One word describes this spot heavy. the wave itself is not that heavy at all but the locals all shred and unless you too rip getting a wave by yourself will be an ordeal. my advice, if it gets crowded and it will stick to the inside peack directly infront of the main peak these waves come out of nowhere and jack up for almost a hundred yards, nothing like the real dona ana but a good crowd alternative.

this spot is a wonderfull alterntive if boca is either not breaking or
crowded. Just watch out for the barnacle encrusted rocks that line the entry/exit point, and the impact zone.

there are two different ways to access dona ana 1) pay the old guy at the park seven dollars(which is a big rip off) or 2) paddle over from Boca Barranca.

#40 – Puerto Caldera

This spot has very very good left located 3 km south of Boca Barranca, Puntarenas.

a rivermouth break with a left breaking at low, incoming tide over a sand bar. This break needs
a large swell from the south/southwest. Just to the south, you will find "El Hoyo" which is a thick, hollow right hand which forms off a jetty and breaks over a sand bar. It is more consistent than Boca Barranca. To get to " El Hoyo," you must enter the port and "convince" the guard to let you through.

Boat or a 4WD and really good road map

Description: Located right off the highway to the left, visible underneath a brdge you cross over shortly after the port. A high quality left which breaks off a jetty and in front of the river mouth.
Tides: Best at a low to mid tide rising.
Swell: Needs a large south/southwest.

CORRALILLO - 5 min form Puntareanas. Follow the road to Jaco, Turn right in Puerto Caldrera, Enter the Port(you have to walk form the entrance to the beach). Then when you are in the beach turn left and walk to the next beach(across the rocks). The last Point. Pay the man in the entrance to Park the Car in the beach (2000 colones)

It's a point break, but in rainy season a river mouth is opened and it gets bigger waves, and also tubes. Watch out in rainy season beacause some times a croc gets out of the river mouth.

EL OLLO - Read the direction in corralillo i the same one but in the entrance of the beach instead of cros-

CENTRAL PACIFIC REGION: SURF MAP

ing to the left walk to the right in a "malecon" nice wave, for beginers is just amazing have very nice size and fun but some times the tide take you to the rocks in front so be careful! sometimes the onshore takes some action there so surf in the morning!

#41 – Tivives

Playa Tivives and Valor Featuring a variety of waves from beach breaks (Tivives) to a rocky point (Valor). Good quality rights and lefts.

Offering a variety of lefts and rights, beach breaks and rocky points (Valor).

Tivives offers rights & lefts breaking with strong currents; the mouth of the river creates and almost perfect, tubular left (beware of crocs & dirty water). Valor is accessed by paddling across the river.
Best at incoming high tide with a south swell (L & S).

ACCESS: On the way to Jaco, instead of taking a right to go to Jaco, go directly like 8 miles, you will see a sign to enter Tivives, from there you take a left on a gravel road for like 4 miles. Ask permission to the guard to enter, just tell him you are going to surf.

The place, on a nice swell and with the right conditions, will give excellent surf-

Puerto Caldera
Photo: Rafael Garita [rafaelgarita@gmail.com]

CENTRAL PACIFIC REGION: JACO BREAKS

ing. The currents are killers so you will need to paddle for a while, even when sitting on the lineup. When it gets to big 10+ it tends to close out. Be careful with the powerful sets because they will for sure kick in with 5 or 6 big waves. If the surf is not that good you can cross the rivermouth and go to Mini Valor which has some nice hollow waves, sometimes perfect tubes.

#42 – Playa Valor

Playa Tivives and Valor Featuring a variety of waves from beach breaks (Tivives) to a rocky point (Valor). Good quality rights and lefts.

#43 – Playa Leon Breaks

Good beach breaks. Ask some locals and go on an adventure! We can't give everything away.

#44 – Playa Escondida

Excellent point break that peaks up forming a very good left and a surfable right. Accessible by land I you are a member of the beach club there (fresh water shower on the beach for member and guests), or by taxi boat to the cove to the south. You can rent a boat from playa Jaco or playa Herradura.

a horseshoe, A-frame reef break with a powerful, hollow left and mellower right. Be aware of low tides as rocks are exposed. Best at mid - high tide with a southwest/west swell. Boat access only from Herradura Bay.
ACCESS: You need to hire a boat in Jaco. The reef and point are at the right of the beach.

Located just north of Jaco possible to drive in, but the only beach access is by a private club. Most people take a boat from Herradura, approx. $20-$40 per person.

#45 – Playa Jaco

Can be good beach break when the surf is not too big. Tends to close out when it gets over 5 feet. Playa Jaco is approximately 2 hours from San Jose(140 km), and the waves are not always dependable. One of its principal attraction has been surfing, this because of its location on the central pacific and it being so close to great quantity of places, specially playa Hermosa, playa Escondida, and Boca Barranca, Puntarenas. Jaco is a growing center of tourism enjoyment, with hotels, cabins and camp grounds.

long beach with lefts and rights breaking and sandbottom and rocks. This area is smaller than
Hermosa and a good option for beginners. Best in front of Cabinas Alice at the south end, in front of Disco in the middle, and in front of Copacabana at the north end.

Description: A 5 km.long beach with lefts and rights breaking over sand and small river rocks. Usually half the size of Hermosa yet gets very peaky and fun. A good alternative to the close out of Hermosa, great for beginner surfers. Best spots are in front of Cabinas Alice

CENTRAL PACIFIC REGION: JACO BREAKS

at the south end, in front of La Central Disco in the middle, and in front of Hotel Copacabana at the north end. Perfect for beginners.

#46 – Roca Loca

Roca Loca Located 1.5 km south of playa Jaco. A rocky point with rights that break over submerged rocks. To get the point, you will have to climb a small hill.

A right which breaks in deep water over a reef. It is one of the heaviest spots on the coast offering long, clean rights. Climb down the cliff just before the highway takes you down into Jaco. Paddle out through a narrow 8" wide channel visible on the inside reef at low tide. Best on a due WEST swell at low to incoming tide.

Description: A deep water right witch breaks over reef in front of small grouping of exposed rocks 50 m. off the cost. One of the heaviest spots on the Pacific Coast. Paddle out through a narrow 8' wide channel visible on the inside reef at low tide. Paddle straight out then veer towards the right as you get past the inside reef section. Takeoff zone is in front of the rocks though you can take off to side of them. Not a very shallow reef yet one must be aware of the tides and takes off positioning. Go first time with a local. Use a bigger board. It is a good indicator of west swell, if it is working chances are other

Playa Escondida
Photo: Shifi
www.shifisurfshots.com

reefs breaks are working.
Tides: Best around a dead low to incoming tide
Swell: Best on a clean west swell.

#47 – Playa Hermosa Breaks

Very strong beach break. This long stretch of break peaks working any given day, but the preferred sand bar is located in front of a large tree known as the Almendro. The waves conditions are generally best when the tide is rising.

Long stretch of beach offering some of the most consistent conditions on the Pacific Coast. A variety of sandbars have formed creating a pounding and tubular beachbreak. The following are the breaks that line this beach:

Terraza - a fast, hollow right breaking in front of a group of visible rocks. Several other breaks just south of this break offer less punishing waves breaking over a sandbar. Best conditions on a west/southwest swell from low to mid tide incoming.

Backyard - a very consistent sandbar located at the entrance to the dirt road in Hermosa. This wave breaks close to the beach and is generally hollow with rights and lefts. Best conditions on a southwest/west swell at mid - high tide incoming.

Almendro (Almond Tree) - breaking in deeper water than most of the hotel breaks, this break also offers a sand-bottom with rights and lefts. Best conditions on a south/southwest swell at mid- high tide incoming.

Corners - breaking in even deeper water creating a little more size, more sand bottom rights and lefts. Generally bigger than northern breaks of Hermosa. Best conditions at low to mid tide and a west/southwest swell.

Tulin - located in front of the Soda Tulin about 10 minutes south of the Backyard, this break is consistently a few feet bigger than the hotel breaks. There is also a rivermouth break further south (with crocodiles) with a perfect line-up in ideal conditions. Best conditions at low tide on a west swell.

Because the surf in Playa Hermosa is more challenging than nearby Jaco, this area attracts a more experienced surfers.

#48 – Estrellos Oeste

Esterillos Este, Esterillos Oeste, Bejuco, Boca Damas. Beach breaks, good wave forms, the points located very close to playa Hermosa, making easy access and many nearby accommodations. The wave conditions are very similar to those of playa Hermosa.

The points of this beach are located very close to Playa Hermosa beach of Jacó. There is easy access and lots of accommodations around. The condition of the waves are also very similar to those of Playa Hermosa with long stretches of break peaks all year round and the best conditions when the tide is rising.

14km South of Hermosa beach, before you get to esterillos centro turn west off main highway drive down a couple km towards small fishing village, theres a

CENTRAL PACIFIC REGION: SOUTH OF JACO

couple smaller resorts north and smells like fish

probably just park your car by the small restaurant where all the toothless fishermen hang out, theres a small cabinas real cheap like
40 yds from beach, smells like fish everywhere, if its not quite big enough to be fun head to esterillos centro you can walk about 25 min
or so. south of mermaid statue at resort down to centro all has little sandbars. good if centro is packed with people.

atmosphere is great fisherman will take you out if you just help them out for a couple hours. great place to stay if on a longer vacation and
need a couple weeks or days to save money and escape the sin pit that is jaco. also good to brush up on espanol skills because theres
very few tourists or english speakers besides small resort north of where the road hits the beach. gorgeous wide white sandy beach can
walk for miles if youre into that.

#49 – Estrellos Este

Esterillos Este, Esterillos Oeste, Bejuco, Boca Damas. Beach breaks, good wave forms, the points located very close to playa Hermosa, making easy access and many nearby accommodations. The wave conditions are very similar to those of playa Hermosa.

#50 – Playa Bejuco

Esterillos Este, Esterillos Oeste, Bejuco, Boca Damas. Beach breaks, good wave forms, the points located very close to playa Hermosa, making easy access and many nearby accommodations. The wave conditions are very similar to those of playa Hermosa.

ACCESS: Stay on the main highway going south out of Jaco towards Quepos and Dominical. Pass Esterillos. About 10-15 min. past Esterillos there will be a bunch of signs directing you down various dirt roads that access the beach. Keep your eyes open because there are lots of these signs. Take the Bejuco sign. Drive down the road and park by the bar on the left.

The wave can be fast and were powerful the morning I surfed it. Very long, hollow, 4-6ft rights. Some lefts got ridden too, but it was predominantly firing right barrels the morning I was there. Lots of paddling once you're in the water in order to track the waves but there's little to no current.

There was a camp ground to the right of where we parked, and a bar on the left. Open beach with no one around (of course we were there at about 6am, so go figure). Very quiet, with not many locals. I was surfing with one local American and one of his buds. You could see the car the whole time, so no need to worry about security or anything like that. There are very rarely shark attacks in Costa Rica due to some fishing incidents they've had recently that killed off a bunch.

A good spot. I don't know the best time of year because I was only in CR for a week in March. I was staying in Esterillos and when it was small, Bejuco was still firing. I can't even imagine what it's like during a big swell. It's around the southern point that's visible from the beach in Esterillos so it benefits from

CENTRAL PACIFIC REGION: SOUTH OF JACO

SW and S swells. It was a fun spot with plenty of barrels to be had for us that day. Whatever SPF sunscreen you use in the states, double it! Even at 7am the sun was starting to burn me.

#51 – Palo Seco

Good beach break. Ask some locals and go on an adventure! We can't give everything away.

Places to Stay around Hermosa

Located just 5 minutes south of Jaco, Playa Hermosa is a small community of surfer friendly hotels and small restaurants. All accommodations are located beachfront with surf right out the door.

BACKYARD HOTEL
This newly built hotel sits right on the beach of Playa Hermosa. This hotel is ideal for those of you looking for surf out your backdoor and nice, relaxing accommodations.

HOTEL FUEGO DEL SOL
Located beachfront in Playa Hermosa, making it a perfect location for checking out the local surf. This small surfer friendly hotel was recently remodeled and under new administration, offering 15 rooms, a private pool, restaurant, bar and private parking.

HOTEL TERRAZA DEL PACÍFICO
The Terraza del Pacifico is a surfer friendly hotel located on the secluded,

Backyard, Playa Hermosa
Photo: Rafael Garita
rafaelgarita@gmail.com

CENTRAL PACIFIC REGION: SOUTH OF JACO

pristine black beaches of Playa Hermosa.

HOTEL VILLA CALETAS
The Villas Caletas is located high on a cliff over the ocean surrounded by rainforest, this tropical mansion and the surrounding private villas provide the ideal getaway for honeymooners/couples to enjoy the beauty of the Central Pacific in a first class environment.

HOTEL MARRIOTT LOS SUEÑOS
The brand new Marriott Los Suenos resort is an incredible resort that offers everything that one could imagine. This 202 room hotel, located only 5 minutes from Jaco has an 18 hole golf course, a private beach/marina, 6 restaurants and lounges, large pool, casino and entertainment center, lighted tennis courts, jogging trails, a 1,100 acre rainforest reserve and much more!

HOTEL FIESTA, BARRANCA
Long lefts at BOCA BARRANCA ALERT!...This beautiful resort comprises 230 rooms in 3 story building, featuring 143 standard rooms with two full size beds and 87 ocean view Jr. Suites with queen size bed and sofa bed.

BEST WESTERN JACÓ BEACH
The Best Western is a beachfront hotel that offers first class lodging in a resort atmosphere.

HOTEL ARENAL PACÍFICO
This new hotel sits beachfront Jaco at the more remote southern end of town. The hotel offers standard and suite rooms that are situated around beautiful gardens, old growth trees, and the local Jaco

Tulin, Playa Hermosa
Photo: Shifi
www.shifisurfshots.com

CENTRAL PACIFIC REGION: MANUEL ANTONIO/ QUEPOS

beach.

HOTEL CLUB DE MAR
Each villa has an ocean view and is designed to provide the concept of indoor/outdoor living in harmony with the surroundings.

Surfing in Manuel Antonio

Manuel Antonio is a beautiful town located about 45 minutes south of Hermosa offering beginner surfers, or, surfers traveling with non-surfing partners, an excellent destination.

Manuel Antonio is one of Costa Rica's most visited destinations. It has it all - from the small town life offered in Quepos to the beautiful beaches of Manuel Antonio.

Manuel Antonio combines breathtaking jungle and ocean views, exotic beaches, unique wildlife, a wide variety of adventure activities, friendly local & tourist community and plenty of restaurants and bars creating an unforgettable experience for travelers of all walks of life.

Although this area is not known as a prime surfer destination (like Jaco, for instance), there are some fun beach breaks at the local beaches and some excellent uncrowded breaks within a short drive.

Getting There
Manuel Antonio is accessed by a paved road (almost completely) from San José (3 hours) or by a shuttle flight into the local airport in Quepos (no boards over 7 feet).

Manuel Antonio caters more to the beginner and moderate surfer, however with a nice swell these local break can be fun for all surfers. Just outside of Manuel Antonio and Quepos you can find some of the nicest and most remote waves in all of Costa Rica.

Best Time: May to November

#52 – Boca Damas
(Boat Access Only)

A very strong, and hollow right. This wave is best at low tide filling in with a mid size to large swell from the northwest or west.

ACCESS: At the rivermouth of the Boca river. Just north of Quepos about 30 minutes

#53 – Quepos

This small left `point is found at the river mouth in the city of Quepos, easy access with many restaurants and accommodations.

A long, perfect left coming off the pier. At low tide, you can catch hollow, strong waves. Needs a large swell to break. Best conditions with a west-northwest swell at low tide. Turd alert: water can be dirty.

#54 – Manuel Antonio

Manuel Antonio Beach break, lefts and rights with good shape. This coastal area needs larger swell for the surf to show.

CENTRAL PACIFIC REGION: MANUEL ANTONIO/ QUEPOS

Manuel Antonio Park
Photo: Marco Lilliu

#55 – Playitas

Manuel Antonio Beach break, lefts and rights with good shape. This coastal area needs larger swell for the surf to show.

A short beach break located at the northern most end of the beach in Manuel Antonio. Best
conditions with a medium to large swell from the south/southwest at mid to high tide. With a
big swell, you can also surf the outer reef with offers long, open rights, ideal for longboarding
by paddling across the river... beware of crocodiles!

Most would park at Manuel Antonio and walk the 100yds or so north past the big rock to this rocky cove. Better access is turning off of Manuel Antonio road at the hotel Mariposa and following this little dirt road down the mountain where you can park on the beach.

Med-high to high tide is best. At this tide however some nasty rocks
that are exposed at lower tides are hidden. Check the place out at low tide to get a fix on the obstacles. ideal for longboarding

If you're hard-core, this is not the wave for you. I found it perfect for me in that I could dawn patrol with my buddy (often the only two out) and be back at our hotel by 8:30 or 9:00 to hook up with the waves and do other activities. If you're travelling with a wife or girlfriend and you want to surf, but it's not the whole purpose of your trip, and you're satisfied with surfing decent-but-not-great waves in an absolutely beautiful environment, then Manuel Antonio and Playitas are a good call.

COSTA RICAN LOVE
Photo: Shifi
www.shifisurfshots.com

CENTRAL PACIFIC REGION: MANUEL ANTONIO/ QUEPOS

#56 – Bajo

A strong, yet short left & right point located just south of Playitas. Best conditions with a small - medium swell from the south/southwest at mid - high tide.

#57 – Playa El Rey

Rights and lefts beach break peaks. Best access to get there is taking the road to playa Dominical, 25 minutes from Quepos, in Roncador go right 11 kms and you will be there.

Very similar to Playa Hermosa; this isolated beach break offers lefts and rights that close out with the presence of a big swell. Always bigger than nearby breaks so if you are in Manuel Antonio with non-surfers and are looking for relief, check this place out. No crowds with several peaks and is only accessible via a palm plantation about 15 minutes south of Quepos.
Best conditions at mid - high tide incoming.

Places to Stay around Quepos

MAKANDA BY THE SEA
The Makanda is a luxury, romantic, adults only hotel offering contemporary Villas and Studios in a quiet jungle setting with a sunset ocean view. Makanda offers open air villas and studios throughout the beautiful jungle property.

HOTEL COSTA VERDE
This hotel offers some of the most spectacular views of the Manuel Antonio National Park and the surrounding beaches and jungle. The hotel offers efficiency rooms.

HOTEL SI COMO NO
Only 5 minutes from the beautiful Manuel Antonio beach and national park, this hotel is in the ideal location for enjoying the sunny beaches and warm waters of Costa Rica.

HOTEL LA MARIPOSA
One of the original hotels in Manuel Antonio. The Mariposa is a luxury hotel that sits on top of the hill in Manuel Antonio minutes from the beach, offering the best ocean views around.

HOTEL VERDE MAR
One of the few beachfront hotels in Manuel Antonio, the Verde Mar is an excellent choice for those of you who would like to have the beach in your back yard and jungles as a backdrop. Economy, standard and suite rooms are available.

TULEMAR BUNGALOWS
The Tulemar is located in the ever popular Manuel Antonio, offering a unique combination of ocean front pleasure and a dreamy mountaintop quality with awe inspiring views of the Pacific Ocean. This hotel's 645 sq. ft. bungalows are scattered.

Surfing in Dominical

Dominical is a good option for those looking for similar conditions to Playa Hermosa in a more relaxed atmosphere. The surf here is mostly beach break, however, tends to close out on bigger swells as it is not as steep as Hermosa. There is a point break just to

CENTRAL PACIFIC REGION: DOMINICAL

the south which offers some good surf on a bigger swell.

Where the Talamanca Mountain Range gently slopes into the South Pacific Ocean and waterfalls cascade down and spill onto the beaches, you will find the small town of Dominical. Dominical, is a small laid back town surrounded by pristine rainforest and beautiful coastlines. This surfer's paradise offers great surf, numerous local restaurants, bars and a wild nightlife.

Dominical is geared towards serious surfers who wish to avoid the heavy crowds of Playa Hermosa and are looking for a more relaxed, tropical atmosphere.

Getting There
Dominical is accessed by a dirt/gravel road from Manuel Antonio (1 hour) which can be accessed by paved road from San José or shuttle flight into the local airport of Quepos.

Reaching Dominical and the surrounding area is easier than one might expect. It is a three and a half hour drive from San Jose by car through some of the most visually stunning scenery in the entire country. Traveling south along the Pan-American Highway below Cartago takes you through the country's largest cloud forest and the worlds last remaining, sustainable habitat, for the endangered quetzal.

The highway between San Jose and San Isidro is best traveled during day light hours, as the fog, rain and mad road conditions make driving difficult during evening hours. While there are still some sections with rather large potholes, the road is in generally good condition. There is an ENORMOUS amount of heavy vehicle traffic on this road (buses, trucks, etc.) so it is recommended you drive with caution. Due to the climb, the temperature at higher elevations is surprisingly low. Make sure to fill your tank before leaving for San Isidro, as there are no gas stations after departing San Jose. As you arrive in San Isidro, approximately 2:45 minutes after departing San Jose, make a right turn after passing the Yamaha dealer on the right side. After veering right, follow this road straight, which continues on towards Dominical. From this point, you are approximately 30-40 minutes away from Dominical. Generally speaking, the road is in fine condition except for a few sections which were washed away during the hurricane of 96'. After a moderate climb, the road heads south rather quickly, en route to the coast. For those interested in heading either north or south from Dominical, it is a one and a half hour drive to Quepos by car; 4x4 recommended. The road south to Punta Uvita has recently been repaved and is in very good condition. It is only necessary to rent a four wheel drive car if you intend to do some exploring in the mountains or continue traveling further north or south.

Best Time: May to November

Dominical is a good option for those looking for similar conditions to Playa Hermosa in a more relaxed atmosphere.

#58 – Playa Matapalo

Good beach break. Ask some locals and go on an adventure! We can't give everything away.

CENTRAL PACIFIC REGION: DOMINICAL AREA

#59 – Playa Guapil

Just 2 miles north of Dominical. Playa Guapil has a great and uncrowded beach-break.

#60 – Dominical

Good, strong beach break with lefts and rights. Beautiful landscapes and very tropical.

Strong beach break with lefts and rights. Fairly consistent break, located about 45 minutes south of Quepos. The northern end of the beach offers bigger sets while the southern end is better for intermediate surfers. Best conditions at mid - high tide.

The Point also known as "Cambutal" is a long, peeling lefthand reefbreak that is rarely too small to surf, and can handle swells up to 15 feet and larger without closing out. When small it's a great wave for beginners, but when it get's big the point is best left to experienced surfers. There's also an "unnamed" wave across the bay-it's a long easy righthander, just right for beginners.

This is Costa Rica's version of Puerto Escondido, so bring more stick than you think you will need. Lots of broken boards.

Great town, good people. This is a surf town but it is much less developed than Jaco and Tamarindo. Other spots in the area give you an alternative to this powerful break. Beautiful scenery. Picture a rain forest meeting the ocean.

Dominical and Baru River
Photo: Rafael Garita [rafaelgarita@gmail.com]

#61 – Dominicalito

Playa Dominicalito is a five minute drive south of Dominical, and is a popular beach for beginning surfers. Waves here are small and gentle – normally about a third the size of Dominical's waves – but there are a few rocks spread out along the bottom so this spot is best surfed at highertides. A pretty beach and a popular weekend spot for Ticos, Playa Dominicalito is also where local fishermen bring in their daily catch.

Places to Stay aound Dominical

HOTEL VILLAS RIO MAR
The Rio Mar is situated on the banks of the Baru river. This jungle resort offers a relaxing environment with first-class hospitality. The resort consists of 40 thatched roof bungalows.

HOTEL ROCA VERDE
A 10-room boutique hotel. The Roca Verde is tucked away in its own secluded cove in Dominical, offering plenty of privacy and seclusion.

#62 – Playa Ventanas

Playa Ventanas is located just south of Marino Ballenas National Park. The easiest way to explore this national park is by accessing it through the town of Uvita, located to the north of the protected zone. Passing south over the Bahía de Coronado will take visitors to Drake Bay and the Osa Peninsula.

Playa Ventanas (Windows Beach) get's it's name from the beautiful sea caves that line the north and south ends of the beach. The two caves on the north-end extend from the beach out to the ocean, a distance of about 50 meters, and during certain tides create a sort of

Dominical Surf Shop
Photo: Francesco Marco

CENTRAL PACIFIC REGION: DOMINICAL AREA

"blowhole" effect. Pressure from each wave blows a large cloud of steam out onto the beach. The caves on the south end of the beach tunnel deeply into the rock, and inspire thoughts of hidden pirate treasure.

Ojochal is located approximately 4 1/2 to 5 hours south of San Jose on the Pan American Highway.

Access: Once you arrive at Dominical you will come to a "T" in the road with a fruit stand and the police check point. You will turn left and head south on the Costanera Sur Highway. It will be the best highway you will have encountered in Costa Rica. Dominical is an immediate right off the highway once you cross over the Rio Baru. Continue south on the Costanera Sur. You will drive about 15 minutes and come to Uvita. From there proceed south another 10-15 minutes and you will come to the "Ventanas de Osa" service station and other stores on your left.

#63 – Playa Ballena

Playa Ballena is located in Marino Ballena National Park, and is one of the best beginner's waves in the area. Long, peeling waves break gentle on the outside, and then roll for a long way in towards the beach. This wave never gets very big, usually only around a third the size of Dominical, and not just a beginners wave but a great longboarding spot as well. Marino Ballena is a stop on the humpback whales migratory routes, and during the winter months, Oct-Mar, it's common to see mother whales, their babies, and adult males breeching the surface

Hotels & Surf Camps

Green Iguana Surf Camp
(Dominical)

Contact info: Web: www.greeniguanasurfcamp.com/ Phone 011(506) 8825-1381 or by email admin@greeniguanasurfcamp.com

Tres Olas Surf Camp
(Playa Guapil)
www.tresolassurfcamp.com/home.htm
rick@tresolassurfcamp.com

Adventure Spanish School
(Dominical)

Contact info: International Tel.: 1-800-237-2730 for world-wide access
E-mail: main@adventurespanishschool.com   Web: www.adventurespanish-school.com

HOTEL DIUWAK
HOTEL AND BEACH RESORT. BAR AND RESTAURANT, San José
TEL: (506) 2280-8907
FAX: (506) 2224-9128
PLAYA DOMINICAL
PHONE: 2787-0087
FAX: 2787-0089
P.O. BOX: 7737-1000 SAN JOSE, COSTA RICA
E-MAIL: reservaciones@diuwak.com

#64 – Punta Uvita

Good beach break. Ask some locals and go on an adventure! We can't give everything away.

CENTRAL PACIFIC REGION: DOMINICAL AREA

#65 – Boca Coronado

Rivermouth break. Ask some locals and go on an adventure! We can't give everything away.

SOUTHERN PACIFIC REGION

Southern Pacific Coast, Osa Peninsula
Photo: Thornton Cohen (www.nomadpics.com)

SOUTHERN PACIFIC REGION

Weather in Southern Costa

What will the weather be like during my vacataion? While the weather man may not always be right, there are some things that you can count on as far as the weather goes in southern Costa Rica. Costa Rica has two weather seasons: the warmer, dry, sunnier season from December to April, and the cooler "green" season, May through November.

Most years, November and December are transition months when the rains become less frequent and the sun shines every day. In the dry season we may not see a drop of rain for the four months of January through April. The skies are blue, the water is crystal clear, and the stars and milky way put on a show at night.

Likewise, April and May are the transition months in which we begin to see evening, then late afternoon showers. These showers start earlier in the day until September and October when it can rain all day every day for weeks-- which is why we are closed during that time. The restaurants close, hiking trails become unsafe due to falling limbs and giant seed pods, and vacations just are not as fun when it's raining all day every day.

Compared to the northern part of Costa Rica, which is dry and almost desert like, the landscape in the southern zone of Costa Rica is very green and lush, and although it does rain here more than in the north, it usually comes as a welcome respite from the heat. Pavones has it's own microclimate. The closest weather station that reports is in Golfito, where it can rain or

Brian Bratton at Matapalo, Osa Peninsula
Photo: Thornton Cohen (www.nomadpics.com)

thunderstorm daily. However, with the benefit of the Conte-Burica range at our back and its position at the mouth of the Golfo Dulce, Pavones has its own unique weather patterns and is generally much sunnier than Golfito.

Southern Pacific Surf Spots

#66 – Drake Bay

Drake's Bay and area Accessible only by boat. This remote break offers long, powerful waves when the swell is running. Boca del Rio Sierpe, is another place with exciting potential for the same kind of waves . Corcovado national park is an adjacent kingdom of lush, tropical wilderness, approximately 1-1/2 hours by boat.

#67 – Carate

Good beach break. Ask some locals and go on an adventure! We can't give everything away.

Surfing in Matapalo

Situated on the extreme tip of the Osa Peninsula, Matapalo offers the extreme adventurer with an opportunity to witness one of the few untouched, pristine regions in Costa Rica. Matapalo combines dense jungles, breathtaking beaches, world class surfing in a peaceful, remote setting. Matapalo offers three excellent point breaks that, with the right swell, will make any traveler unpack, and stay a while.

However, there are several downsides to staying in Matapalo. First of all, the surf is not very consistent. Second, because this area is one of Costa Rica's few remaining pristine destinations, the "locals," (which in this case, any American who got there before you), are not very welcoming to new faces. Also, it is important to mention that this area is extremely remote and all power here is provided by solar energy. There are no restaurants, bars, shops and therefore, all hotels include all meals in their stay (which means rustic accommodations, does not mean "rustic" prices!

Located across the bay from Pavones, the Matapalo area catches the same swells, but is much less surfed and provides excellent waves for a variety of skill levels.

The first beach is called "Pan Dulce" which means sweet bread in spanish, and is perfect for beginners! On a normal swell, the inside break there is a small nice wave to learn how to surf. On the outside break you can perfectly find the point break and with big swell you can surf it all the way to the shore. Almost one and a half minute surfing the same wave!

The next beach to the southwest is called "Backwash". This beach offers a nice sand break at low tide with a fast and steep wave. On normal conditions it is very safe but on big swells it gets up to 10 feet and should not be surfed by those with limited experience.

The beach that is the furthest west is named "Matapalo". It offers exciting and very challenging surf for the most experienced surfers. This break holds the largest swells in the area but also more rocks. Under normal conditions

SOUTHERN PACIFIC REGION

waves are up to 25 feet and it is safe to surf, but watch out for those rocks!

Access to Matapalo is via a paved road from San José all the way down south (there are some sections towards the end that are not paved…4x4 recommended) or via a shuttle flight to the local airport of Puerto Jimenez and then a one hour cab ride into Matapalo.

Best Time: May to November
World class surfing in a peaceful, remote setting. Finicky, though.

#68 – Cabo Matapalo

Excellent right points located in front of Pavonnes, you can get there by road from Pavonnes or by car from Golfito. Perfect waves.

A powerful, and steep right hand wave that breaks best at mid tide offering fast rides. Because it faces the open ocean, it picks up more swells & is more consistent than nearby breaks. Best conditions at mid tide and a west/southwest swell.

Drive past pavones, backwash and its the next break visible.

Park in the parking lot, and surf it during middle or high tide. It is for experienced surfers only. Matapalo is one of 4 point breaks there. Pan Dulce is the first you drive by. Very gentle longboard wave most days, hits at low tide. Next is Backwask: holds amazingly large swell. Next is Matapalo-it is the ultimate wave. Large group of rocks on the inside. Finally (and much less surfed, working only on high tide becvause of very dangerous rocks) "the Crack", which is basically the headland point of the Osa Penninsula.

Sunset session
Photo: Thornton Cohen (www.nomadpics.com)

SOUTHERN PACIFIC REGION: SURF MAP

Starting at the Crack and working back, each break will be a bit smaller. These are all relatively rocky breaks BUT if there is a good south swell the place is amazing (and amazingly crowded with highly territorial locals.) It is true that there are a lot of ex-pats that live there that think they own it. Huge egos abound. VERY expensive lodging and very little of it. Only one cantina nearby. It is about 10 hours dive from SJ. You must drive through 3 rivers so if it rains hard you are not leaving till the water subsides.

Puerto Jimenez is a very rough Tico fishing village. I have been there many times and have had some of my favorite surf trips there. It is very hit and miss but it is absolutely the most beautiful place I have ever seen. Monkeys and parrots in the trees everywhere. It is not a bad place just to be, surf is a bonus. So the skinny is: very expensive, few lodging choices, inconsistent rocky breaks with the potential for occasional "world-class" surf, territorial locals, lots of surfers, beautiful place.

CHECK IT AT:
www.costaricasurfguide.com/matapalo.htm

#69 – Backwash

A large, yet slow right that breaks over a reef in the middle of breathtaking Backwash Bay. Due to the steep beach, the waves generally jack up creating steep sections; great longboarding.
Not as consistent as Matapalo, however, when it is going off, outshines Matapalo. Best conditions from mid-low tide and south/west swell.

Backwash - A fun right that breaks in the middle of Backwash Bay.
Although it doesn't break as many days per year as Matapalo, it is the spot of choice when it is at its best (from midtide to lowtide).

CHECK IT AT:
www.surf-costarica.com/break/backwash.htm

#70 – Pan Dulce

A long right powerful point break that needs a large swell to work. With ideal conditions, you can expect up to 500 yd tubular rides. This wave has several fast sections that break over a rocky bottom. Best conditions with a large swell from the south at mid tide.

A few points before Matapalo...just before backwash

This wave has several fast sections that break over a rocky bottom. Best conditions with a large swell from the south at mid tide. Get it good and you won't want to leave. Most beautiful part of costa rica...monkeys in the trees, clear blueish water, and a perfect point break.

CHECK IT AT:
www.surf-costarica.com/break/pan_dulce.htm

Places to Stay

This area is extremely remote and all power here is provided by solar energy. There are no restaurants, bars, shops and therefore, all hotels include all

SOUTHERN PACIFIC REGION: PAVONES

meals in their stay.

HOTEL BOSQUE DEL CABO
Bosque del Cabo with its private, cliff top bungalows is a romantic getaway and a naturalist's dream come true. Private spacious bungalows offer beautiful ocean views, tropical breezes and the rainforest at your doorstep.

HOTEL LAPA RIOS
This secluded luxury resort consists of 14 private comfortable cabinas that are surrounded by the lush rain forests of the Osa Peninsula. This area is home to its own private 1000 acre private reserve.

ENCANTA LA VIDA LODGE
Encanta La Vida is in the deep jungle where there is the highest density of wildlife in all of Costa Rica - and that's saying a lot. The Casona suitable for families and larger groups.

Surfing in Pavones

Pavones is one of Costa Rica's most famous surf breaks offering one of the world's longest lefts which, on a good day, can connect for 2 - 3 minute rides. The wave has several sections which allow for carving, pumping and, of course, showing off for the folks sipping on their Imperials at the Cantina at the end of the break. This area is extremely remote and if you can catch it on a good day, the logistical nightmares surrounding your arrival will be well worth it.

However, there are many things to

Surfers watch a sunset session at Pavones
Photo: Thornton Cohen (www.nomadpics.com)

SOUTHERN PACIFIC REGION: PAVONES

consider before traveling to Pavones. Due to its location on the interior of the Golfo Dulce, it is blocked from many swells and can go for weeks with no surf. Moreover, once the swell hits, it is common to see a large crowd of international travelers (+ the protective locals) battling for position. We recommend not going here until you know there is surf... because once you get there, it's a long way back!

The surf season in Pavones runs from March through August. During this time, there can be swells of up to 12 feet hitting the top of the point, at the more advanced section of the wave. This is no spot for beginners, as the wave is fast and crowded with experienced surfers. We teach lessons in the bay next to the cantina where the wave height can be 1/2 the size of the waves on the outside point.

Our surf camp season starts in December when the waves are more gentle, forgiving, and perfect for learning. If you've never surfing before, the months of December through February are for you. Not only will you experience the sunniest skies of the year, but you'll also be surfing in conditions better suited for beginner surfers.

Getting There
Access to Pavones is achieved via a paved road all the way down south or fly into Golfito (no
boards over 7ft) and catch a cab down to Pavones.

Best Time: May to November
This area is extremely remote and if you can catch it on a good day, the logisti-

Pavones Line
Photo: Thornton Cohen (www.nomadpics.com)

cal nightmares surrounding your arrival will be well worth it.

#71 – Playa Pavonnes

Excellent left point, considered one of the longest in the world. Good shape and very fast. It is located 400 kms from San Jose (8 hours by car). Bring camping gear if you wish to hang there. Out on the peninsula across Pavonnes, a half-hour boat ride away, there is a series of right points (Matapalo) the equivalent of Pavonnes world class lefts.

Pavones is situated in the 'deep-south' of Costa Rica, on the southern side of the Gulfo Dulce, nearest town of any size (!) Golfito. Six to eight hours from San Jose. Pavoness is 2 hrs south of Golfito,theres bus service and 4x4 cabs,theres also 2 Sansa flights from San Jose,for about 60$ each way,its pristine Costa Rica, Golfito is super hot,the drive is beautiful,passing teak plantations,lowland rainforest and crossing about dozen rivers.

The wave needs a BIG southern swell, as the set up is a long wrap around on a 'Raglan' like beach of boulders. This is a great wave if you catch it when it is working. It goes on forever, supposedly it is the second longest lefthander in the world. Rumours suggest that Kelly Slater has a house close by (like how many other places in the world??)

Pavones is one of the best left points in the world theres also breaks south to punta banco lefts and rights,the natural beauty of this place is indescribable,at night everyone hangs out at the cantina,theres great fishing ofshore,and 3 excellent breaks on the other side,of the bay.

It is a great place if the wave is working, but you are out in the middle of nowhere if it is not. A small number of 'surf related' amenities exist for accomodation etc. The wave can get crowded when its working. - word gets around fast!

#72 – Punta Banco

Punta Banco is a reef break with rights and lefts located just south of Pavones. Good place to check out if Pavones is too small or too crowded. Best conditions at mid to high tide with a swell from the south, or west.

#73 – Punta Burica
(Boat Access Only)

Welcome to the end of the world. Very, remote & powerful reef breaks located on the very tip of Costa Rica on the border of Panama. Best conditions with a swell from the south or SSW.

Where to Stay around Pavones

There are very few hotels in the area and almost no services.

This area is extremely remote and all power here is provided by solar energy. There are really no restaurants, bars, shops to speak of and therefore, all hotels include all meals in their stay.

CABINAS MIRA OLAS
Spacious cabins with kitchen and pri-

vate bath in a jungle setting above the pavones´surf break.
It´s location allows easy access to the beach and stores.

CABINAS LA PONDEROSA
La Ponderosa offers 5 cabins with view of the ocean, private bathrooms with hot water, ceiling fans, accommodating up to 4 people. 3 of those cabins have a/c. You will find a separate dining area and recreation area as well.

CASA SIEMPRE DOMINGO
Located up in the mountain, this hotel offers 4 large rooms with private bath. Each room offers
a double beds or 2 double beds and one single bed.

Recommended Pavones Surf Camps & Schools

VENUS SURF ADVENTURES
http://venussurfadventures.com

CARIBBEAN REGION

Gnarly Caribbean Surf, not for the faint of heart
Photo: Casey Rossi

CARIBBEAN REGION: PUERTO LIMON AREA

Puerto Limon Surf Spots

#74 – North East Breaks

Good beach break waves accessible via Tortuguero channels or by private plane. You can rent a boat to take you through the channels near Puerto Moin, 15 km north of playa Bonita.

#75 – Los Tumbos

Get it good and you won't want to leave. Most beautiful part of costa rica...monkeys in the trees, clear blueish water, and a perfect point break.

#76 – Portete

A small bay located north of playa Bonita. With a right working off the southerly point. Since it is close to Limón, you will find easy access.

#77 – Playa Bonita

A point/reef break known for its very thick, powerful and dangerous left. Located 5 km north of Limón (downtown).

#78 – Isla Uvita (Boat Access Only)

An island off the coast of Limon. Here you will find a good left. Isla Uvita is about a 20 minutes boat ride from Limon with passage available at certain times of the year.

This island located off the coast of Limon offers an excellent, yet, dangerous left that breaks on a reef. This is most powerful left in Costa Rica with three sections and facing a coral reef.
Best days offer waves with 10 ft faces and is accessible only by boat from Limon.

Los Tumbos
Photo: John L. Lyman

CARIBBEAN REGION: SURF MAP

#79 – Westfalia

A stretch of beach breaks extending south from Limón to Cahuita, offering lefts and rights that tend to close out where the swell gets too big.

#80 – Playa Grande (Cahuita)

Decent beach break north of Playa Negra. You can walk to Negra but you'll probably want to drive to Playa Grande. Dont confuse this Playa Grande with the one north of Tamarindo, which is typically MUCH better.

#81 – Playa Negra (Cahuita)

Black Beach, Cahuita An excellent beach break, not well known and therefore not heavily visited. Nevertheless, there are waves all year round.

#82 – Cahuita Park

Very small and good for beginners mostly. Just south of town in the park.

Puerto Viejo

Puerto Viejo is a laid back village that moves to a reggae beat. Beaches - never crowded, surfing, snorkeling, biking, wildlife, hiking, excellent restaurants, and friendly people can make this your favorite vacation spot. (Most people return once they have visited Puerto Viejo.) Puerto Viejo is a fun, inexpensive place to spend a month, week or weekend.

Puerto Viejo has certainly most known for being home to what has been called the heaviest wave in Costa Rica: Salsa Brava. Salsa, although fickle, has definitely earned this reputation offering a thick "sauce" breaking over a shallow reef. The wave is very competitive and certainly, for experts only. More intermediate surfers can check out the beach break just south at Playa Cocles.

The Caribbean coast is quite different than the Pacific as you will find it is not as nearly built up and the culture/atmosphere is even more laid back than other parts of Costa Rica.
Getting There

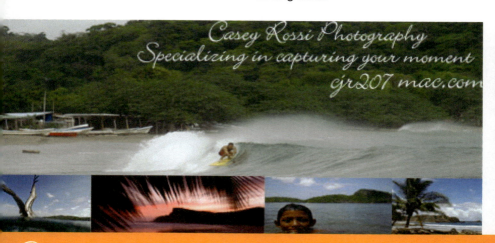

CARIBBEAN REGION: SURFING PUERTO LIMON

Drive 2 hours east from San José until you reach Limon and take a right and continue for one hour until you reach Puerto Viejo

Best Time: November to March
Puerto Viejo is an ideal location for laid back surfers and travelers looking to avoid the more commercialized Pacific coast.

#83 – Playa Negra (Puerto Viejo)

Decent to great beach break depending on the swell. Can be consistent. Just in town on the north end. Can't miss it.

#84 – Salsa Brava

A very thick and voluminous wave that comes from deep water onto a shallow reef, also called "salsa", for its juice power. This place gets very big and tubular (legitimate big wave). Salsa is approximately a 3-1/2 hour drive from San Jose and there is a restaurant and accommodation close to the point.

A thick Hawaiian style wave that builds in deep water and breaks over a shallow reef. Offers both lefts and rights, however the right is generally faster, with a steep entry. This is most powerful wave in Costa Rica and the best conditions with an easterly swell which can produce up to triple over-

Getting Barrelled on Playa Negra (Puerto Viejo)
Photo: Casey Rossi

CARIBBEAN REGION: CAHUITA

head surf.

#85 – Playa Cocles

This beach break offers a more consistent break with lefts and rights breaking close to the beach. This wave tends to jack up with a big swell due to the steep beach entry ...beware of currents. Best conditions in the early morning before the winds blow it out. However, you can surf here all day as the wind often improves the lack of form.

#86 – Playa Chiquita

Fun beach break.

#87 – Manzanillo

A very fast beach break located 20 km from Puerto Viejo, Limon. Here you find rustic lodging and typical food. Located close to an unpaved road, and easy to get to

#88 – Punta Mona

Good point break if its working

Caribbean Shore Pound
Photo: John L. Lyman

CARIBBEAN REGION: PUERTO VIEJO

#89 – Playa Gandoca

Fun beach break.

Where to Stay around Puerto Viejo

There are a variety of accommodations in Puerto Viejo, however, we recommend heading just south to Cocles.

VILLAS DEL CARIBE
The Villas del Caribe consist of twelve fully equipped villas located amidst a coconut grove, on the beach and combine maximum enjoyment of nature with utmost comfort, cleanliness and safety.

CASA CAMARONA LODGE
The Casa Camarona offers eighteen guest rooms that are beautifully appointed in the rustic style of the Costa Rican Caribbean.

EL PIZOTE LODGE
Set about 10 walking minutes west of the town Puerto Viejo on a quiet backroad, just across from the black beach. All rooms are spacious and have two double beds, ceiling fans and hot water.

SIA TAMI LODGE
A rustic but amiable lodge of 10 houses build in the most authentic Caribbean style, respecting the environment and integrating perfectly in the idyllic landscape.

Make sure to check out our **Blue Planet Nicaragua Surfing Guide** for details on where to surf in Nicaragua:

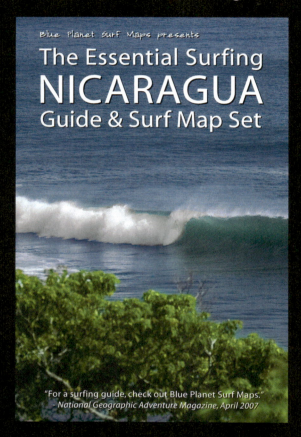

- 82 Pages of Advice
- Full Color
- Lots of Maps
- Photos to get stoked!